STEPHEN CRANE
in the West and Mexico

STEPHEN CRANE

in the West and Mexico

EDITED BY JOSEPH KATZ

The Kent State University Press

For the benefit of
his friends by
CK.
Jan. 1895
Mr. S. Crane starts. WEST.
on a journalistic tare.

This drawing by Corwin Knapp Linson is from a copy in the collection of Joseph Katz. Linson, an illustrator, was one of Crane's circle during his New York days.

Copyright © 1970 by Joseph Katz.
All rights reserved.
Standard Book Number 87338–094–0.
Library of Congress Catalog Card Number 73–106970
Manufactured in the United States of America
by Edwards Brothers, Incorporated.
First Edition
Designed by Merald E. Wrolstad.

To the memory of my mother
Sadie Strumwasser Katz

Acknowledgements

I am indebted to Edwin H. Cady, Matthew J. Bruccoli, and Harry R. Warfel for reading and commenting upon various stages of this work. To Fredson Bowers and Bernice Slote I owe debts of gratitude for various courtesies, including the exchange of information. Kenneth A. Lohf, Curator of Special Collections of the Butler Library, Columbia University, has been extremely generous in aiding my use of the rich resources in his care; and William A. Runge and Anne Freudenberg, of the Alderman Library, University of Virginia, were most helpful whenever I had occasion to use materials they secure. I am additionally grateful to Hyman W. Kritzer, Director of Kent State University Libraries, and Dean H. Keller, Assistant Director, for the several services of a library hospitable to scholarship. I wish to acknowledge permission from Alfred A. Knopf, Incorporated, owners of the literary rights to Stephen Crane's writings, to use certain material within their control. My constant debt is to Karen, for being Karen.

J. K.

Contents

Introduction

These seventeen newspaper articles form a sequel to *The Red Badge of Courage*. Stephen Crane wrote them on the occasion of a trip he made early in 1895, about a year after he had completed the novel and while it was being considered for book publication. It had drawn the attention of a publisher by its success as a serial distributed by the Bacheller, Johnson & Bacheller newspaper syndicate. Now the syndicate itself planned to capitalize on that success by paying Crane's bills as he wrote his way along a lightning tour through the West and South, down to central Mexico. Eventually Crane drew on this trip for "The Blue Hotel," "The Bride Comes to Yellow Sky," and other short stories; immediately, however, it resulted in these fourteen dispatches and three "Mexican Tales."

Uneven in quality as travel sketches, they are primarily important because they record Crane's progress as a man and an artist, revealing him engaged deeply in a role much like the one he had created for the protagonist of his Civil War novel. Like Henry Fleming before Chancellorsville, Stephen Crane before this journey was essentially unfinished. The formal education he ended prematurely in 1891 had been only minimally relevant to him, and the following years he spent as a newspaperman and freelance writer were limited in ways that begin in geography. For example, to the point at which he started his tour, Crane was fundamentally an Easterner. With a childhood and young manhood spent in New Jersey, Pennsylvania, and New York, his experiences were rooted in the tri-state region that has New York City as its cultural center. His formulation of the larger world had of necessity been purely imaginative. This journey was his first away from the East, and it served him in much the same way Henry Fleming was served by his army experiences—as a rough equivalent of the *grand tour*, as an occasion on which the unfamiliar forced him to confront himself and his understandings.

Crane seems to have begun thinking of this kind of trip several years earlier, apparently inventing it as an escape from an unpleasant situation. When he left Syracuse University in June, 1891, he had gone to work for his brother's New Jersey Coast News Bureau. In college he had boasted about Townley working for the New York *Tribune* and being a member of the Press Club, but after a year he seems to have concluded that what he had once seen as the big time really was very small.[1] By the summer of 1892, several of the Jersey Shore reports he was writing for the *Tribune* began to satirize Asbury Park and its founder, James A. Bradley. As this continued a catastrophe of some kind became inevitable. The one that came resulted from the column published on 21 August. Four days before, the Junior Order of United American Mechanics paraded through the Methodist resort community. Crane reported the parade with a biting sketch in which the ragged line of shabby workmen came off much better than the idlers who watched them with amusement. But the *Tribune's* owner, Whitelaw Reid, was Benjamin Harrison's vice presidential running-mate, and the opposition found it possible to misrepresent the report as anti-labor. There was a tempest that was capped on 24 August, when a member of the J.O. U.A.M. wrote the *Tribune* that its sketch was un-American. Crane wrote his proposal for the tour on the next day. To the manager of the American Press Association he bluffed: "I am going south and, also, west this fall and would like to know [if] I could open a special article trade with you. I have written special articles for some years for the Tribune and other papers. Much of my work has been used by the various press associations; and I would like to deal directly with you if possible. Kindly let me know if it would be worth my while to send you copy for consideration."[2]

---

[1] Frederic M. Lawrence, "The Real Stephen Crane," an unpublished memoir in the Katz collection.

[2] Crane to the manager of the American Press Association, 25 August 1892; published in R. W. Stallman and Lillian Gilkes, *Stephen Crane: Letters* (New York, 1960), p. 11.

But the fall of 1892 saw Crane a stringer for the New York City newspapers, his travels restricted to wanderings from one temporary lodging to another. In the next two years, however, his situation had changed. By the fall of 1894 he had passed to the limits of his apprenticeship as a writer and he became well-known on Park Row. He had written, published, and paid for *Maggie: A Girl of the Streets* (1893); although it did not sell he had used it wisely to court Hamlin Garland, William Dean Howells, and others whose favor might do him some good. In 1894, when Copeland & Day, the noted *avant garde* publishing house, took his second book, *The Black Riders and Other Lines* (1895), the stage was set for something grand. Irving Bacheller recognized that thing in the manuscript of *The Red Badge of Courage:* he not only committed his syndicate to distribute the novel as a serial, but he also took on other work by Crane. "Billie Atkins Went to Omaha" (published too as "An American Tramp's Excursion") suggests that Crane still had his mind on the trip he devised two years earlier. Now it was possible.

He and Bacheller evidently had decided upon it by the middle of September 1894, but they had set no firm departure date. Crane wrote Copeland & Day that he expected to leave on "November 20th or about then," but he didn't go. Thomas Beer says he wrote someone else, "Bacheller thinks I had best start for Nevada as soon as possible, maybe before Christmas, but I should like to be with the family, of course."[3] Again and again his letters drag in reference to the impending trip. Finally, around 28 January 1895, he left New York for the "west to write sketches with a free hand, as long as he finished the trip in Mexico."[4] Corwin Knapp Linson's drawing, "Mr. S. Crane starts WEST on a journalistic tare," suggests that there had been a high-spirited going-away party to send him off in good style.

[3]Crane to Copeland & Day, [27 September 1894?], in Dean H. Keller, "Stephen Crane to Copeland & Day: A New Letter," *Stephen Crane Newsletter,* II (Fall 1967), 7. Beer, *Stephen Crane: A Study in American Letters* (New York, 1923), p. 110.

[4]Beer, *Stephen Crane*, p. 112.

Dependent on the railroads, he "passed comet-wise through Philadelphia," bid a hasty farewell to his friend Dr. Frederic M. Lawrence, continued west to Chicago, and paused. There, according to Beer, "His impressions . . . were stained by a procession of Lord Fauntleroys met on a corner beside a church. That any young male should be draped in lace and velvet and made to wear long curls!" He was in Cooke's European Hotel in St. Louis by 30 January, and the next day he wrote his friend Lucius L. Button:

> St. Louis
> Thurs—
> Hello, Budge, I am en route to kill Indians. Before I left I called upon you at the place where I thought I was most likely to find you. Write to me at Lincoln in care of Mr Will Owen Jones of the State Journal.
> Lincoln, Nebraska, I mean.
> My distinguished consideration.
>
> > Yours as ever
> > Crane[5]

He reached Lincoln the following day, 1 February. There the newspapers greeted him soberly. The *Evening Call* noted that "Stephen Crane arrived in Lincoln yesterday as the representative of a syndicate of prominent eastern newspapers, to write up the true condition of the drouth-stricken west." With a good deal more detail the *State Journal* explained that much was at stake on the results of the visit: "Stephen Crane, representing a large syndicate of newspapers of national reputation and influence, arrived in Lincoln last evening, drawn to the state by the distressing special dispatches sent out of Omaha to advertise the drouth. Mr. Crane's papers have asked him to get the truth, whether his articles are sensational or not, and for that reason his investigation will doubtless be welcomed by the business interests of Nebraska."[6]

---

[5] Lawrence, "The Real Stephen Crane." Beer, *Stephen Crane*, p. 112. Crane to Button is in the Alderman Library, University of Virginia, and is first published here.

[6] Lincoln *Evening Call*, 2 February 1895, p. 5; Nebraska *State Journal* 2 February 1895, p. 6. A clipping of the *State Journal* notice is in Crane's scrapbook in Special Collections of the Columbia University Libraries. See

Obviously, whether or not he had suspected it, Crane had arrived in the midst of a Situation. Farmers in a large area of Nebraska had been thrice devastated. In the summer of 1894 they had suffered heat, drought, and violent winds that turned the soil into dust. The staggering loss of crops was followed that winter by the wholesale death of livestock starved through lack of fodder and frozen by exceptionally harsh blizzards. Many families emigrated; those who remained needed help if they were to survive. Nellie Bly reported all this for the New York *World*, and Robert B. Peattie of the Omaha *World-Herald* reinforced what she had said. Assistance came. Then—third disaster—the issue became muddied. Nebraska business interests feared that Eastern investors would shy away from a state that lived in so perilous a relationship with nature. They wanted it made clear that a large part of the state was unaffected. And there was greed and corruption in the local aid distribution centers, with news of this creating far-from-local cynicism about what was happening out there. Eastern papers like the Philadelphia *Press* were mingling stories of hardship with others of malfeasance. If, as seemed likely, help dwindled as a result of these stories, the men who battled for their farms would have to abandon all hope.

Crane saw the story and wrote it that way, resolving statistics with color through a focus on the fundamental point that bad things were happening to admirable people who did not deserve defeat. He not only interviewed officials in the state capitol, he also rode the two hundred miles to Eddyville, a little town in north central Nebraska, to see the people and learn their pain. A blizzard that struck on Wednesday, 6 February, caught him in Eddyville and helped him experience a small part of it. When he returned to Lincoln soon after 9 February, he wrote "Nebraska's Bitter Fight for Life," the first, and one of the most successful, of the journey sketches. Occasionally overwritten, it is saved from bathos by Crane's firm stance, his clear vision, and his ability to capture hard, ironic, frontier humor. The result is an affirmation of human

---

also Bernice Slote, "Stephen Crane in Nebraska," *Prairie Schooner*, XLIII (Summer 1969), 192–199.

courage in the face of crushing forces. In that respect it is tied to
the slum fiction Crane had written during the preceding two years.
Now he was witnessing part of what he had trained himself to
understand during his apprenticeship, modifying that understanding to embrace a larger area of the human condition. Modified still
further by his experiences in the Commodore's dinghy two years
later, it would develop into the theme of "The Open Boat" and
"The Five White Mice."

There are, however, unsettling accounts of Crane in Lincoln.
Thomas Beer reported something odd that happened on 13 February. The scene is a barroom that R. W. Stallman places in the
Hotel Lincoln: "It appears that a very tall man was pounding a
rather small one and Crane shoved himself between them. 'But
thus I offended a local custom. These men fought each other every
night. Their friends expected it and I was a darned nuisance with
my Eastern scruples and all that. So first everybody cursed me
fully and then they took me off to a judge who told me that I was
an imbecile and let me go; it was very saddening. Whenever I try
to do right, it don't.' "[7] Possibly apocryphal, the story nevertheless
is of a piece with another account of Crane in Lincoln. Using the
pen name "Henry Nicklemann," Willa Cather wrote as a memorial the only eye-witness record of Crane on his journey.[8] She was a
student at the University of Nebraska and a part-time staff member of the *State Journal*, and he was out of money, stranded in
Lincoln until Bacheller wired more.

It was on the last night he spent in Lincoln. I had come back from

[7] Beer, *Stephen Crane*, pp. 113–114. Stallman, *Stephen Crane: A Biography*
(New York, 1968), pp. 130, 132. Stallman's account differs in details from
Beer's, although it offers no evidence that is based on a source other than
Beer: Here the brawl takes place on 12 February and the courtroom
appearance is on 13 February. Stallman, however, also sets the Eddyville
trip after 13 February and is positive about other matters for which he cites
no evidence.

[8] "When I Knew Stephen Crane," *The Library*, 23 June 1900, pp. 17–18.
The essay appeared two weeks after Crane's death. It was republished in
Prairie Schooner, XXIII (Fall 1949), 231–236. For an evaluation of

the theatre and was in the Journal office writing a notice of the play. It was eleven o'clock when Crane came in. He had expected his money to arrive on the night mail and it had not done so, and he was out of sorts and deeply despondent. He sat down on the ledge of the open window that faced on the street, and when I had finished my notice I went over and took a chair beside him. Quite without invitation on my part, Crane began to talk, began to curse his trade from the first throb of creative desire in a boy to the finished work of the master. . . . In all his long tirade, Crane never raised his voice: he spoke slowly and monotonously and even calmly, but I have never known so bitter a heart in any man as he revealed to me that night. It was an arraignment of the wages of life, an invocation to the ministers of hate.

When Crane "came in from the streets to write up what he had seen there, his faculties were benumbed, and he sat twirling his pencil and hunting his words like a schoolboy. . . . He declared that his imagination was hide bound; it was there, but it pulled hard. After he got a notion for a story, months passed before he could get any sort of personal contract with it, or feel any potency to handle it." But, of course, that was not possible on this trip.

These are glimpses of a man who is beginning to lose composure. In the past two years Crane evidently had learned to blend into the varied backgrounds of New York City. As he moved through its demimonde, soaking in the material of his writings, he must have encountered situations similar to the barroom brawl reported by Beer—situations which must have had even greater possibilities for danger had he blundered in the same way. Evidently he had not blundered then; perhaps he had developed the ability to sense the nature and requirements of such situations, perhaps he simply had learned that the first rule of survival at this level was to not butt in. His blunder now suggests that he was off-balance. Willa Cather's remarkable account offers substantiation of that. Possibly both a cause and a symptom of imbalance was the number of times Crane ran out of money during his three months of travel. Broke in Lincoln (according to Cather), he was (according to Dr. Lawrence)

Cather's memoir, see Bernice Slote, "Stephen Crane and Willa Cather," *Serif*, VI (December 1969), 3–20.

broke again in New Orleans, again (according to Thomas Beer) in San Antonio, and again (according to a telegram from Bacheller) in Mexico City. [9] This was a remarkable performance even for one so heedless of expenses as Stephen Crane. Perhaps it helps to explain his preoccupation with the cost of things in all of the sketches but "The Fête of Mardi Gras," an idyll. Certainly his sketches after "Nebraska's Bitter Fight for Life" increasingly focus on externals and decreasingly show what one critic found in the Nebraska piece —"the presence of an informing, creative intelligence that could select, organize, and show as one experience this very clutter of separate things." [10]

Crane left Lincoln on or around Thursday, 14 February, his departure announced by the *State Journal:*

> Mr. Stephen Crane of the New York Press and the Bacheller & Johnson syndicate has finished his work in Nebraska and will next visit New Orleans, the southwest and Mexico in search of picturesque material for special articles. It so happened that he was out in Dawson county at the time of the blizzard and he felt that he had material for a thrilling story. When he returned to civilization and found that he could have met a meaner blizzard at about the same date if he had remained in New York, his disgust was copious enough to fill a furniture van. [11]

On his way to New Orleans, however, he passed through Hot Springs, Arkansas. "Seen at Hot Springs" departs from the not-very-curious fact that visitors to the Arkansa resort gambol in a sempiternal Spring. The Jersey Shore report three years earlier led to this trip because in it Crane bitterly satirized vacationers in a playground much like the one he was in now, but this piece rambles to a close with a biteless anecdote about a barroom con game.

A few days later, Crane was in New Orleans. [12] The bustle and

---

[9] "Nicklemann," " When I Knew Stephen Crane." p. 18. Lawrence. "The Real Stephen Crane." Beer, *Stephen Crane*, p. 115. Bacheller to Crane, 25 March 1895, in the Butler Library, Columbia University.

[10] Slote, "Stephen Crane in Nebraska," p. 195.

[11] Nebraska *State Journal*, 14 February 1895, p. 4. Reprinted in Slote, "Stephen Crane in Nebraska," p. 195.

[12] Stallman (*Stephen Crane: A Biography*, p. 113) asserts that Crane arrived in New Orleans on 16 February, moved from a boardinghouse to the hotel

excitement of the city as it filled for the Mardi Gras caught him almost immediately. On 19 February he wrote a fractured foreign language letter to Linson: "Friedweller die schoñenberger je suis dans New Orleans. Cracked ice dans Nebraska, terra del fuego dans New Orleans. Table d'hotes sur le balconies just like spring. . . . Frequented I all the time here again l'etoile de Virginitie sur St Louis Street. Sic semper tyrannis! Mardi gras tres grande but it does not until next Tuesday begin. Spiel!"[13] He filled in his time before the Mardi Gras by playing—by attending the French Opera Company's performances of Jacques Halevy's *La Juive* on the evening of 20 February, and *La Fille de Madame Angot* on Sunday evening, 24 February, or Thursday afternoon, 28 February. Crane's "Grand Opera in New Orleans" is a guide book account of the company he projected as a model for operatic repertory groups. When the Philadelphia *Press* published it, an editor chopped two paragraphs out of the middle and two paragraphs off the end—and for more than seventy years no one seemed to recognize that it had been mutilated.[14] But Crane now seems to have wished more for a holiday than for the excitement and conflict that can lend interest to travel

---

Royal on 20 February, and then wrote the Nebraska sketch. But in the absence of supporting evidence, this must be judged unlikely. I have searched the *Times-Democrat* and the *Picayune*—the major New Orleans papers—for February and March without finding announcements of Crane's arrival or departure from the city. Neither paper reports him in the Royal or any other hotel during that time. (A. C. H. Crane of Newark arrived in the Cosmopolitan on 13 February, according to the *Picayune's* list the next day, but this could not have been Stephen Crane.) And since the Nebraska sketch appeared as early as 23 February ("Nebraska's Fight," New Orleans *Times-Democrat*) with cuts distributed by Bacheller, Johnson & Bacheller, it must have been written and sent to New York before the third week in February.

[13]Crane to Linson, "Tuesday" [19 February 1895], in the Syracuse University Library. Published in Edwin H. Cady and Lester G. Wells, eds., *Stephen Crane's Love Letters to Nellie Crouse* (Syracuse, 1954), p. 8. (The letter is reproduced on pp. 12–13 of that book.)

[14]See, for example, George Monteiro, "'Grand Opera for the People': An Unrecorded Stephen Crane Printing," *Papers of the Bibliographical Society of America*, XLIII (First Quarter 1969), 29–30. Monteiro noted that *Public Opinion*, XVII (4 July 1895), 770, quoted from the Galveston *News* appearance several lines not in the *Press*, but thought "it is doubtful that the three sentences can be attributed to Crane."

sketches. The difficulties that plagued the French Opera Company after their manager resigned come through in the articles that began in the New Orleans papers shortly before Crane arrived and continued after he left.[15] After implications that Mr. Arthur Durieu, the company's manager, had mishandled its funds, he resigned. Management was assumed by the tenor, L. Anasty, president of the Association of French Opera Artists, who immediately repudiated the season coupons sold by Durieu. Some members of the company had not been paid for three months, and Durieu was unable to account for the sales of the coupons. This was just the "ear-splitting row" Crane denied hearing. "The Fête of Mardi Gras" suggests that he simply did not want to hear it. He wanted peace. The reasons for this are evident in the articles that followed.

On Thursday, 7 March, the Galveston *Daily News* published a brief note of welcome:

> Mr. Stephen Crane, representing the New York Press and the Bacheller & Johnson syndicate arrived from New Orleans yesterday morning, and will spend some time in Galveston gathering materials of an interesting and historical character concerning Galveston and vicinity to be published in the papers served by the syndicate. Mr. Crane is regarded as one of the brightest and most entertaining special writers of the day.[16]

However, the posthumously-published "Galveston, Texas, in 1895" only uses the city as the occasion for a discussion of Crane's increasing discomfort with the tourist's point-of-view. "In a word," he summarized, "it is the passion for differences which has prevented a general knowledge of the resemblences." But the humor with which the piece develops is forced and the wit is brittle.

Beer made an observation that may be pertinent here. "He could not report," he said of Crane. "Apparently he did not even try to report. Of what use to any newspaper was an impression of

---

[15]As, for example, in the following *Times-Democrat* articles: "French Opera," 16 February 1895, p. 3; "French Opera," 17 February 1895, p. 3; "The French Opera," 19 February 1895, pp. 4, 7.

[16]"Personal," Galveston *Daily News*, 7 March 1895, p. 4. The "Hotel Arrivals" reports Crane as in the Tremont, one of the city's best hotels.

impatient horses kicking 'grey ice of the gutter into silvery angles that hurtled and clicked on frozen stone' when the boy had been sent to get the facts of a large and important fire." Now, however, facts were increasingly overpowering the "informing, creative intelligence that could select, organize, and show as one experience this very clutter of separate things." Probably it was this that made one of Crane's friends say, many years later, "he had made a poor fist of his stories—statistics and ordinary matter—which he was doing for the Bacheller Newspaper Syndicate."[17] The Galveston sketch suggests that Crane was aware of this, and concerned by it. Unlike the New York City sketches that had preceded this trip, his writings now tend to reflect a narrator without the ability to project a firm relationship to situations. No doubt this reflected Crane's own response to the stresses that accompanied his writing: in little more than a month he had rushed through some of the most individualistic communities in this country; now he was pushing on from Galveston to San Antonio to Mexico. For one who until then had been no closer to the Pike County of frontier myth than the very real, and very tame, Pike County in Pennsylvania, his tour must have been a kaleidoscope of the unfamiliar.

The evening on which he intended leaving for Mexico Crane wrote a second letter to Lucius L. Button. In contrast with the playfulness of the earlier "I am en route to kill Indians," this one sounds depression: "I would tell you of many strange things I have seen if I was not so bored with writing of them in various articles."[18] He actually left on 17 March, five days later than he had planned. Looking back on the trip in the first "Stephen Crane in Mexico" article, he projected himself not as a cowboy or frontiersman but, ruefully, as an archaeologist. Evidently the theorizing of the Galveston sketch had not solved his problem.

---

[17]Beer, *Stephen Crane*, p. 82; Slote, "Stephen Crane in Nebraska," p. 195; Nelson Greene, "I Knew Stephen Crane," an unpublished memoir in the Public Library of Newark, New Jersey.

[18]Crane to Button, 12 March 1895; published in Stallman and Gilkes, *Letters*, p. 54. But the Butler Library has Crane's passenger check for the trip from San Antonio to Laredo, and it is dated 17 March.

"The Main Streets of this City," one of the City of Mexico dispatches, shows it at its extreme. Here the telling of fact, scene, and
event in guidebook fashion, without a shaping vision, has resulted
in a narration that is almost completely disembodied. Its source is a
seeing-machine planted in the streets, and its coherence is based
on the associations suggested by what that machine chances to see.
For that reason transitions are haphazard and the sequence of
material is arbitrary. The first two paragraphs suggest that the
theme of the sketch will be a contrast between the chaotic order of
the North and the placid unpredictability of Mexico's capital, but
this theme is weakened in transition to the third paragraph, and it
is an increasingly slender thread thereafter. From weather to
women, to the buildings from which women peer, to architectural
organicism, to *ubi sunt* reflections on particular buildings, to the
influence on commerce by North Americans, to the triumph of an
American circus over the natives, to menace in the faces of bull-
fighters, then to an equivalent portentousness in the priests who
pass through the streets. This is the product of a fatigued mind
forced to work beyond its abilities to modify preconceptions, jum-
bling verities and uncertainties as it labors on to fulfill an obligation.

Then, somehow, came "The Viga Canal." During the nine
weeks he spent in Mexico, Crane seems to have tried to sample
everything: in addition to the shops, restaurants, and places of
amusements around the Hotel Iturbide he saw the *Corrida de
Beneficencia* from a seat in the more expensive shady section of
the ring, he bought the first five fractions of a ticket in the Loteria
Nacional of 27 April, and—as earlier he had secured a guest pass to
Galveston's Aziola Club—he managed the use of a non-active
membership card issued "From April 1895" to E. M. Larranaga of
Tehuantepec for the Mexican Athletic Club.[19] On 30 March he
wrote a friend: "This is to say that I am well and am going to

---

[19]Souvenirs of Crane's trip are in the Butler Library, Columbia University.
The bill from the Hotel Iturbide is difficult to decipher. It reads as if it were
for a stay of thirty days divided into two periods of fifteen days ending on
15 May 1895.

ascend Popocatapetl. Whether I will be well afterward is a matter of speculation."[20] It was probably around this time that he spent a day on another tourist sidetrip, the boat ride through the Viga Canal to the village of Santa Anita and the Floating Gardens.

In "The Viga Canal" the journey and return provide unity and coherence for one of the finest sketches Crane wrote during his trip. It begins with a cab ride from the hotel in the center of Mexico City to the embarkation point in the southeastern section. The two miles to Santa Anita are telescoped into a few short paragraphs in which references to Popocatepetl and Ixtaccihuatl suggest the boat's progress. After a focus on the village scenes, it concludes with the boat's return—severely foreshortened—past the twin peaks to Mexico City. That is the continuity by which Crane develops a view of a pre-industrial culture economically dependent on exploiting its natural setting and its people, alternating with other views of a Nature that is aloof, independent of man, unalterably following its own order. From this alternation develops a contrast between man and Nature: humanity is inconsequential, squalid, and perverted; Nature is magnificently indifferent, supremely forceful as it looms outside of man's influence. Man (and, with two musicians in his boat to serenade his return, Crane includes himself in this indictment) has but two fundamental aspirations. The first is mundane—economic, material, and sensual—represented by the beggars, the boatman and passengers who collaborate in frivolous races, and the vendors of "melons, saints, flowers." The second aspiration is superstitious, symbolized by the "stern, unapproving" little white church of Santa Anita, a structure that is both "a reproach and a warning" to the foolish. The portentousness implied in several of the journey dispatches and stated in "The Main Streets of this City" is the dominant tone of "The Viga Canal." But now it is sounded under control. Here there is a unifying vision providing integrity to a developing *Naturmystik*. That vision is of a universe which—as a poem in *War Is Kind*

---

[20] Crane to Wickham W. Young, 30 March 1895; published in Stallman and Gilkes, *Letters*, p. 55.

declares—has no sense of obligation to man; it underlines the final contrast between the narrowly-averted collision of the boats and the regular splendor of the stars.

"Above All Things" helps to explain how such an effective piece came out of a journey in which Crane's powers seemed more and more to be out of his control. This is the way a man who needs to resolve himself takes stock. For Crane it meant returning to the problem he had considered in the Galveston sketch. Now he recognized that for him the problem was not one of aesthetics alone: something about men had been bothering him. As he moved further along on his journey he found greater difficulty in understanding the people he found at the bottom of the societies he found. He had no trouble with the Nebraska farmers, poor as they were: they struggled against their fate. But the foreign poor, especially the Mexican Indians, gave another and less attractive face to the human condition. They neither struggled nor protested. They existed, passively. Despite his Galveston principles, Crane viewed them as aliens, ultimately less than people. In several of the sketches they are presented as brutes and beasts of burden—dumb, animal, motivated by instincts Crane could not see himself sharing. But in "A Jag of Pulque is Heavy" he briefly made an illuminating connection between these people and those he had earlier delineated in *Maggie* and the New York City sketches: "The Indian, in his dusty cotton shirt and trousers, his tattered sombrero, his flapping sandals, his stolid dark face is of the same type . . . that is familiar to every land, the same prisoner, the same victim."

This insight is the heart of "Above All Things," a document that is at once the most personal and the most credible of Crane's expositions of his creeds. It is obvious in his other explanations of himself that there is some element of pose before the women and the editorial enquirers to whom he was then writing. Here he seems to have been writing mainly to himself. In "Above All Things" he transforms Christian apostolicity into a revolutionary manifesto for the social millenium that still later culminated in his poem "The Blue Battalions." And here he is a realist who pursues "psychological perceptions" in a universe that is defined morally as well as aesthetically. But it is clear that for him morality is not at all based on traditions of behavior. Just as in Galveston he suggested that truth in art involves cultural relativity and point of view, he now implies that morality is a complex notion based on economy, freedom, and self-denial. The way in which Crane establishes these principles demonstrates an irony that is at once self-reflexive and anti-bourgeois.

Around the middle of May his trip was over, and he was back East. "The one time I remember him talking animatedly and at length was when he returned from his trip to Mexico," his niece recalled.

> The family just at that time consisted of my father, mother, we three girls, the sawyer, the wheelwright, and two men that helped with the farm work. He had us all enthralled. I remember him strumming on a guitar, or banjo, the next day and murmuring, "Magnificent! Magnificent!" as he recalled a religious procession he had seen. However, he never talked about the trip again that I heard, though I often wished he would.[21]

Corwin Knapp Linson saw his excitement too:

> Just as abruptly as he had departed, in so far as I was concerned, just so abruptly he returned. One evening I was alone. A knock at the door brought me face to face with Steve. That evening was a riot of talk. For once his tongue found freedom. . . . From his pocket he handed me a half dozen or more opals, with the lam-

[21] Edith Crane to Louis Zara, 14 December 1958, in the Rare Book Room of the Ohio State University Library. The date of Crane's return is as hazy as the date of his departure. In *Contacts* (New York, 1935), p. 261, Curtis Brown records the inscription in a copy of *The Black Riders and Other Lines* Crane gave him in New York soon after the trip ended: "To Curtis Brown—not at all reluctantly but with enthusiasm—from Stephen Crane, May 16, 1895." But see note 19 for the date of Crane's bill from the Hotel Iturbide, and compare Beer's story (*Stephen Crane*, p. 119) that Crane was in Mexico City when the New York *Herald* reviewed the book of poems, and Corwin Knapp Linson's (*My Stephen Crane*, ed. Edwin H. Cady [Syracuse, 1958], pp. 86, 88) conflicting recollections that Crane was in New York in April and May.

bent flame of sunsets in their depths. He freely gave me the choice of the lot.[22]

His trip had both drained Crane and recharged him. On 8 June he wrote Copeland & Day, "I returned from Mexico some days ago but have come up here for a time because I am not in very good health."[23] And yet during this time after his return he probably was writing the three fables Bacheller sold as "Mexican Tales." In them Crane attempted to write of some lessons he had learned in the past few months: man is complex—crafty, ingenious, untrustworthy, admirable, depraved, exploitive; Nature is immutable, yet susceptible of manipulation; between man and his environment there is a natural tension, with each being unable to dominate the other, except temporarily. Here is the root of the theme that runs through much of Crane's later fiction.

He continued to draw on the trip until he died. In England he delighted to show off and shoot the revolver he had bought with Bacheller's money, and it hung with his spurs, blanket, and assorted other memorabilia in his study. The West and Mexico also play a significant role in his work. In addition to the explicitly Western and Mexican stories that formed a considerable group of his later writings, he remembered what he saw on occasions such as his landing in Ponce, Puerto Rico, during the last phase of the Spanish-American War three years later.[24] But even as one recognizes the externals of the 1895 journey in stories like "The Blue Hotel" and "The Bride Comes to Yellow Sky" one can find in them as well the results of the more significant progress Stephen Crane made then.

---

[22] Linson, *My Stephen Crane*, pp. 87, 88–89. Both Linson and Beer (*Stephen Crane*, p. 119) say that Crane was given the opals by Charles Gardener, who was, according to Beer, "An American engineer, invalid after smallpox. . . ."

[23] Published in Stallman and Gilkes, *Letters*, p. 58.

[24] "The Wonders of Ponce," Kansas City *Star*, 21 August 1895, p. 5. It is published in Matthew J. Bruccoli, ed., Joseph Katz, intro.; "Stephen Crane's First Puerto Rican Dispatch," *Stephen Crane Newsletter*, IV (Fall 1969), 1–3.

In the *Whilomville Stories* and in "The Veteran," Henry Fleming is the man who has solved himself. His growth to maturity involved successive stages in which his preconceptions were established, then shaken, then tested against his experiences, and finally modified to conform more closely with his insight into reality. The process involved psychic and intellectual humbling: eventually Henry "discovered his own actual futility." His creator experienced much the same things during his 1895 "journalistic tare."

Joseph Katz

Columbia, South Carolina

Travel Sketches

1. Nebraska's Bitter Fight for Life

Eddyville, Dawson Co., Neb., Feb. 22.—
The vast prairies in this section of Nebraska contain a people who are engaged in a bitter and deadly fight for existence. Some of the reports telegraphed to the East have made it appear that the entire State of Nebraska is a desert. In reality the situation is serious, but it does not include the whole state. However, people feel that thirty counties in pain and destitution is sufficient.

The blot that is laid upon the map of the state begins in the north beyond Custer county. It is there about fifty miles wide. It slowly widens then in a southward direction until when it crosses the Platte river it is over a hundred miles wide. The country to the north and to the west of this blot is one of the finest grazing grounds in the world and the cattlemen there are not suffering. Valentine is in this portion which is exempt. To the eastward, the blot shades off until one finds moderate crops.

In June, 1894, the bounteous prolific prairies of this portion of Nebraska were a-shine with the young and tender green of growing corn. Round and fat cattle filled the barnyards of the farmers. The trees that were congregated about the little homesteads were of the vivid and brave hue of healthy and vigorous vegatation. The towns were alive with the commerce of an industrious and hopeful community. These mighty brown fields stretching for miles under the imperial blue sky of Nebraska had made a promise to the farmer. It was to compensate him for his great labor, his patience, his sacrifices. Under the cool, blue dome the winds gently rustled the arrays of waist-high stalks.

Then, on one day about the first of July there came a menace from the southward. The sun had been growing prophetically more fierce day by day, and in July there began these winds from the south, mild at first and subtle like the breaths of the panting countries of the tropics. The corn in the fields underwent a preliminary quiver from this breeze burdened with an omen of death. In the following days it became stronger, more threatening. The farmers turned anxious eyes toward their fields where the corn was beginning to rustle with a dry and crackling sound which went up from the prairie like cries.

Then from the southern horizon came the scream of a wind hot as an oven's fury. Its valor was great in the presence of the sun. It came when the burning disc appeared in the east and it weakened when the blood-red, molten mass vanished in the west. From day to day, it raged like a pestilence. The leaves of the corn and of the trees turned yellow and sapless like leather. For a time they stood the blasts in the agony of a futile resistance. The farmers helpless, with no weapon against this terrible and inscrutable wrath of nature, were spectators at the strangling of their hopes, their ambitions, all that they could look to from their labor. It was as if upon the massive altar of the earth, their homes and their families were being offered in sacrifice to the wrath of some blind and pitiless deity.

The country died. In the rage of the wind, the trees struggled, gasped through each curled and scorched leaf, then, at last, ceased to exist, and there remained only the bowed and bare skeletons of trees. The corn shivering as from fever, bent and swayed abjectly for a time, then one by one the yellow and tinder-like stalks, twisted and pulled by the rage of the hot breath, died in the fields and the vast and sometime beautiful green prairies were brown and naked.

In a few weeks this prosperous and garden-like country was brought to a condition of despair, but still this furnace-wind swept along the dead land, whirling great clouds of dust, straws, blades of grass. A farmer, gazing from a window, was confronted by a swirling tempest of dust that intervened between his vision and his scorched fields. The soil of the roads turned to powder in this tempest, and men travelling against the winds found all the difficulties of some hideous and unnatural snow storm. At nightfall the winds always vanished and the sky which had glistened like a steel shield became of a soft blue, as the purple shadows of a merciful night advanced from the west.

These farmers now found themselves existing in a virtual desert. The earth from which they had wrested each morsel which they had put into their mouths had now abandoned them. Nature made light of her obligation under the toil of these men. This vast tract was now a fit place for the nomads of Sahara.

And yet, for the most part, there was no wavering, no absence of faith in the ultimate success of the beautiful soil. Some few despaired at once and went to make new homes in the north, in the south, in the east, in the west. But the greater proportion of the people of this stricken district were men who loved their homes, their farms, their neighborhoods, their counties. They had become rooted in this soil, which so seldom failed them in compensation for their untiring and persistent toil. They could not move all the complexities of their social life and their laboring life. The magic of home held them from traveling toward the promise of other lands. And upon these people there came the weight of the strange and unspeakable punishment of nature. They are a fearless folk, completely American. Their absolute types are now sitting about New England dinner tables. They summoned their strength for a long war with cold and hunger. Prosperity was at the distance of a new crop of 1895. It was to be from August to August. Between these months loomed the great white barrier of the winter of 1894–95. It was a supreme battle to which to look forward. It required the profound and dogged courage of the American peoples who have come into the west to carve farms, railroads, towns, cities, in the heart of a world fortified by enormous distances.

The weakest were, of course, the first to cry out at the pain of it. Farmers, morally certain of the success of the crop, had already gone into debt for groceries and supplies. The hot winds left these men without crops and without credit. They were instantly confronted with want. They stood for a time reluctant. Then family by family they drove away to other states where there might be people who would give their great muscular hands opportunity to earn food for their wives and little children.

Then came the struggle of the ones who stood fast. They were soon driven to bay by nature, now the pitiless enemy. They were sturdy and dauntless. When the cry for help came from their lips it was to be the groan from between the clenched teeth. Men began to offer to work at the rate of twenty-five cents a day, but, presently, in the towns no one had work for them, and, after a time, barely anyone had twenty-five cents a day which they dared invest in labor. Life in the little towns halted. The wide roads, which had once been so busy, became the dry veins of the dead land.

Meanwhile, the chill and tempest of the inevitable winter had gathered in the north and swept down upon the devastated country. The prairies turned bleak and desolate.

The wind was a direct counter-part of the summer. It came down like wolves of ice. And then was the time that from this district came that first wail, half impotent rage, half despair. The men went to feed the starving cattle in their tiny allowances in clothes that enabled the wind to turn their bodies red and then blue with cold. The women shivered in the houses where fuel was as scarce as flour, and where flour was sometimes as scarce as diamonds.

The cry for aid was heard everywhere. The people of a dozen states responded in a lavish way and almost at once. A relief commission was appointed by Gov. Holcomb at Lincoln to receive the supplies and distribute them to the people in want. The railroad companies granted transportation to the cars that came in loaded with coal and flour from Iowa and Minnesota, fruit from California, groceries and clothing from New York and Ohio, and almost everything possible from Georgia and Louisiana. The relief commission became involved in a mighty tangle. It was obliged to contend with enormous difficulties.

Sometimes a car arrives in Lincoln practically in pawn. It has accumulated the freight charges of perhaps half a dozen railroads. The commission then corresponds and corresponds with railroads to get the charges remitted. It is usually the fault of the people sending the car who can arrange for free and quick transportation by telegraphing the commission in Lincoln a list of what their car, or cars, contain. The commission will then arrange all transportation.

A facetious freight agent in the East labelled one carload of food: "Outfit for emigrants." This car reached the people who needed it only after the most extraordinary delays and after many mistakes and explanations and re-explanations. Meanwhile, a certain minority began to make war upon the commission at the expense of the honest and needy majority. Men resorted to all manner of tricks in order to seduce the commission into giving them supplies which they did not need. Also various unscrupulous persons received donations of provisions from the East and then sold them to the people—at a very low rate it is true, but certainly at the most obvious of profits. The commission detected one man selling a donated carload of coal at the price of forty cents per ton. They discovered another man who had collected some two thousand dollars from charitable folk in other states, and of this sum he really gave to the people about eight hundred dollars. The commission was obliged to make long wars upon all these men who wished to practice upon the misery of the farmers.

As is mentioned above, this stricken district does not include in any manner the entire State of Nebraska, but, nevertheless, certain counties that are not in the drought portion had no apparent hesitation about vociferously shouting for relief. When the State Legislature appropriated one hundred and fifty thousand dollars to help the starving districts, one or two counties in the east at once sent delegations to the capital to apply for a part of it. They said, ingenuously, that it was the state's money and they wanted their share of it.

To one town in the northern part of the state there was sent from the East a carload of coal. The citizens simply apportioned it on the basis of so much per capita. They appointed a committee to transport the coal from the car to each man's residence. It was the fortune of this committee finally to get into the office of a citizen who was fairly prosperous.

"Where do yeh want yer coal put?" they said, with a clever and sly wink.

"What coal?"

"Why, our coal! Your coal! The coal what was sent here."

"Git out 'a here! If you put any coal in my cellar I'll kill some of yeh."

They argued for a long time. They did not dare to leave anyone out of the conspiracy. He could then tell of it. Having failed with him, they went to his wife and tried to get her to allow them to put the coal in the cellar. In this also they were not successful.

These are a part of the difficulties with which the commission fights. Its obligation is to direct all supplies from the generous and pitying inhabitants of other states into the correct paths to reach the suffering. To do this over a territory covering many hundreds of square miles, and which is but meagrely connected by railroads, is not an easy task.

L. P. Ludden, the secretary and general manager of the commission, works early and late and always. In his office at Lincoln he can be seen at any time when people are usually awake working over the correspondence of the bureau. He is confronted each mail by a heap of letters that is as high as a warehouse. He told the writer of this article that he had not seen his children for three weeks, save when they were asleep. He always looked into their room when he arrived home late at night and always before he left early in the morning.

But he is the most unpopular man in the State of Nebraska. He is honest, conscientious and loyal; he is hard-working and has great executive ability. He struggles heroically with the thugs who wish to filch supplies, and with the virtuous but misguided philanthropists who write to learn of the folks that received their fifty cents and who expect a full record of this event.

From a hundred towns whose citizens are in despair for their families, arises a cry against Ludden. From a hundred towns whose citizens do not need relief and in consequence do not get it, there arises a cry against Ludden. The little newspapers print the uncompromising sentence: "Ludden must go!" Delegations call upon the governor and tell him that the situation would be mitigated if they could only have relief from Ludden. Members of the legislature, prodded by their rural constituents, arise and demand an explanation of the presence in office of Ludden. And yet this man with the square jaw and the straight set lips hangs on in the indomitable manner of a man of the soil. He remains in front of the tales concerning him; merely turns them into his bureau and an explanation comes out by the regular machinery of his system, to which he has imparted his personal quality of inevitableness. Once, grown tired of the abuse, he asked of the governor leave to resign, but the governor said that it would be impossible now to appoint a new man without some great and disastrous halt of the machinery. Ludden returned to his post and to the abuse.

But in this vast area of desolated land there has been no benefit derived from the intrigues and scufflings at Lincoln, which is two hundred miles away from the scene of the suffering. This town of Eddyville is in the heart of the stricken territory. The thermometer at this time registers eighteen degrees below zero. The temperature of the room which is the writer's bed-chamber is precisely one and a half degrees below zero. Over the wide white expanses of prairie, the icy winds from the north shriek, whirling high sheets of snow and enveloping the house in white clouds of it. The tempest forces fine stinging flakes between the rattling sashes of the window that fronts the storm. The air has remained gloomy the entire day. From other windows can be seen the snowflakes fleeing into the south, traversing as level a line as bullets, speeding like the wind. The people in the sod-houses are much more comfortable than those who live in frame dwellings. Many of these latter are high upon ridges of the prairie and the fingers of the storm clutch madly at them. The sod-houses huddle close to the ground and their thick walls restrain the heat of the scant wood-fire from escaping.

Eddyville is a typical town of the drought district. Approaching it over the prairie, one sees a row of little houses, blocked upon the sky. Most of them are one storied. Some of the stores have little square false-fronts. The buildings straggle at irregular intervals along the street and a little board side-walk connects them. On all sides stretches the wind-swept prairie.

This town was once a live little place. From behind the low hillocks, the farmers came jogging behind their sturdy teams. The keepers of the three or four stores did a thriving trade. But at this time the village lies as inanimate as a corpse. In the rears of the stores, a few men, perhaps, sit listlessly by the stoves. The people of the farms remain close in-doors during this storm. They have not enough warm clothing to venture into the terrible blasts. One can drive past house after house without seeing signs of life unless it be a weak curl of smoke scudding away from a chimney. Occasionally, too, one finds a deserted homestead, a desolate and unhappy thing upon the desolate and unhappy prairie.

And for miles around this town lie the countless acres of the drought-pestered district.

Some distance from here a man was obliged to leave his wife and baby and go into the eastern part of the state to make a frenzied search for work that might be capable of furnishing them with food. The woman lived alone with her baby until the provisions were gone. She had received a despairing letter from her husband. He was still unable to get work. Everybody was searching for it; none had it to give. Meanwhile he had ventured a prodigious distance from home.

The nearest neighbor was three miles away. She put her baby in its little ramshackle carriage and traveled the three miles. The family there shared with her as long as they could—two or three days. Then she went on to the next house. There, too, with the quality of mercy which comes with incredible suffering, they shared with her. From house to house she went pushing her baby-carriage. She received a meal here, three meals here, a meal and a bed here. The baby was a weak and puny child.

During this swirling storm, the horses huddle abjectly and stolidly in the fields, their backs humped and turned toward the eye of the wind, their heads near the ground, their manes blowing over their eyes. Ice crusts their soft noses. The writer asked a farmer this morning: "How will your horses get through the winter?"

"I don't know," he replied, calmly. "I ain't got nothing to give 'em. I got to turn 'em out and let 'em russle for theirselves. Of course if they get enough to live on, all right, an' if they don't they'll have to starve."

"And suppose there are a few more big storms like this one?"

"Well, I don't suppose there'll be a horse left round here by ploughin' time then. The people ain't got nothin' to feed 'em upon in the spring. A horse'll russle for himself in the snow, an' then, when th' spring rains comes, he'll go all to pieces unless he gets good nursin' and feedin'. But we won't have nothin' to give 'em."

Horses are, as a usual thing, cheaper in this country than good saddles, but at this time, there is a fair proportion of men who would willingly give away their favorite horses if they could thus insure the animals warm barns and plenty of feed.

But the people cannot afford to think now of these minor affections of their hearts.

The writer rode forty-five miles through the country, recently. The air turned the driver a dark shade, until he resembeled some kind of a purple Indian from Brazil, and the team became completely coated with snow and ice, as if their little brown bodies were in quaint ulsters. They became dull and stupid in the storm. Under the driver's flogging they barely stirred, holding their heads dejectedly, with an expression of unutterable patient weariness. Six men were met upon the road. They strode along silently with patches of ice upon their beards. The fields were, for the most part, swept bare of snow, and there appeared then the short stumps of the corn, where the hot winds of the summer had gnawed the stalks away.

Yet this is not in any sense a type of a Nebraska storm. It is phenomenal. It is typical only of the misfortunes of this part of the state. It is commensurate with other things, that this tempest should come at precisely the time when it will be remarkable if certain of the people endure it.

Eddyville received a consignment of aid recently. There were eighty sacks of flour and a dozen boxes of clothing. For miles about the little village the farmers came with their old wagons and their ill-fed horses. Some of them blushed when they went before the local committee to sign their names and get the charity. They were strong, fine, sturdy men, not bended like the Eastern farmer but erect and agile. Their faces occasionally expressed the subtle inner tragedy which relief of food and clothing at this time can do but little to lighten. The street was again lively, but there was an elemental mournfulness in the little crowd. They spoke of the weather a great deal.

Two days afterward the building where the remainder of the relief stores had been put away burned to the ground.

A farmer in Lincoln county recently said: "No, I didn't get no aid. I hadter drive twenty-five miles t' git my flour, an' then drive back agin an' I didn't think th' team would stand it, they been poor-fed so long. Besides I'd hadter put up a dollar to keep th' team over night an I didn't have none. I hain't had no aid!"

"How did you get along?"

"Don't git along, stranger. Who the hell told you I did get along?"

In the meantime, the business men in the eastern part of the state, particularly in the splendid cities of Omaha and Lincoln, are beginning to feel the great depression resulting from extraordinary accounts which have plastered the entire state as a place of woe. Visitors to the country have looked from car windows to see the famine-stricken bodies of the farmers lying in the fields and have trod lightly in the streets of Omaha to keep from crushing the bodies of babes. But the point should be emphasized that the grevious condition is confined to a comparatively narrow section of the western part of the state.

Governor Holcomb said to the writer: "It is true that there is much misery in the state, but there is not the universal privation which has been declared. Crop failure was unknown until 1890 when the farmers lost much of their labor, but at that time, and in 1893, when a partial loss was experienced, the eastern half of the state was able to take care of the western half where the failure was pronounced.

"This year has been so complete a failure as to reduce many to extreme poverty, but I do not think that there are more than twenty per cent. at present in need. Great irrigation enterprises that are now being inaugurated will, no doubt, eliminate the cause of failure in large districts of the western part of the state. The

grain that is produced and stock that is raised in this state put it in
the front rank of the great agricultural commonwealths. I have no
doubt that in a year or two her barns will be overflowing. I see
nothing in the present situation nor in the history of the state as I
have observed it for sixteen years that ought to discourage those
who contemplate coming here to make homes. In the western part
of the state, a vast amount of unwise speculation has caused great
losses, but that part of the country cannot be excelled for grazing,
and irrigation will, no doubt, render it safe and profitable for agri-
culture. In the greater part of the state, the people are suffering no
more than a large percentage of the agricultural districts of other
states. It has been brought about as much by the general national
depression as by local causes."

It is probable that a few years will see the farms in the great
Platte river valley watered by irrigation, but districts that have not
an affluence of water will depend upon wind-mills. The wells in
this state never fail during a drought. They furnish an abundance
of cool and good water. Some farmers plan to build little storage
reservoirs upon the hillocks of the prairie. They are made by simply throwing up banks of earth, and then allowing cattle to tram-
ple the interiors until a hard and water-tight bottom is formed. In
this manner a farmer will be in a degree independent of the most
terrible droughts.

Taking the years in groups of five the rainfall was at its lowest
from 1885 to 1890 when the general average was 22.34 inches. The
general average for 1891, 1892 and 1893 was 23.85 inches. But
1894 now enters the contest with a record of but 13.10 inches.
People are now shouting that Nebraska is to become arid. In past
years when rainfalls were enormous they shouted that Nebraska
was to become a great pond.

The final quality of these farmers who have remained in this
portion of the state is their faith in the ultimate victory of the land
and their industry. They have a determination to wait until nature,
with her mystic processes, restores to them the prosperity and
bounty of former years. "If a man stays right by this country, he'll
come out all right in the end."

Almost any man in the district will cease speaking of his woes to recite the beauties of the times when the great rolling prairies are green and golden with the splendor of young corn, the streams are silver in the light of the sun, and when from the wide roads and the little homesteads there arises the soundless essence of a hymn from the happy and prosperous people.

But then there now is looming the eventual catastrophe that would surely depopulate the country. These besieged farmers are battling with their condition with an eye to the rest and success of next August. But if they can procure no money with which to buy seed when spring comes around, the calamity that ensues is an eternal one, as far as they and their farms here are concerned. They have no resort then but to load their families in wagons behind their hungry horses and set out to conquer these great distances, which like walls shut them from the charitable care of other and more fortunate communities.

In the meantime, they depend upon their endurance, their capacity to help each other, and their steadfast and unyielding courage.

2.   Seen at Hot Springs

Hot Springs, Ark., March 3.—
This town arises to defeat a certain favorite theory of all truly great philosophers. They have long ago proven that spring is the time

SEEN AT HOT SPRINGS | [rule] | Crane Writes of a Pictur- | esque Winter Resort. | [rule] | THE JOYS OF INVALIDISM | [rule] | Bath Houses that Are Like the | Abode of Subdued Millionaires— | A Town Not Tender, | But Tolerant. | [rule] | (Copyright, 1895, by Bacheller, Johnson & Bacheller.)

when human emotion emerges from a covering of cynical darkness and becomes at once blithe and true. They have decided that the great green outburst of nature in the spring is essential to the senses before that mighty forgetfulness, that vast irresponsibility of feeling, can come upon a man and allow him to enjoy himself.

The Hot Springs crowd, however, display this exuberance in the dead of winter. It has precisely the same quality as the gaiety of the Atlantic Coast resorts in the dead of summer. There is then proven that the human emotions are not at all guided by the calendar. It is merely a question of latitude. The other theory would confine a man to only one wild exuberant outbreak of feeling per year. It was invented in England.

As soon as the train reaches the great pine belt of Arkansas one becomes aware of the intoxication in the resinous air. It is heavy, fragrant with the odor from the vast pine tracts, and its subtle influence contains a prophecy of the spirit of the little city afar in the hills. Tawny roads, the soil precisely the hue of a lion's mane, wander through the groves. Nearer the town a stream of water that looks like a million glasses of lemon phosphate brawls over the rocks.

And then at last, at the railway station, comes that incoherent mass of stage drivers and baggagemen which badges all resorts, roaring and gesticulating, as unintelligible always as a row of Homeric experts, while behind them upon the sky are painted the calm turrets of the innumerable hotels and, still further back, the green ridges and peaks of the hills. Not all travellers venture to storm that typical array of hackmen; some make a slinking detour and, coming out suddenly from behind the station, sail away with an air half relief, half guilt. At any rate, the stranger must circumnavigate these howling dervishes before he can gain his first glance of the vivid yellow sun-light, the green groves and the buildings of the springs.

When a man decides that he has seen the whole of the town he has only seen half of it. The other section is behind a great hill that with imperial insolence projects into the valley. The main street was once the bed of a mountain stream. It winds persistently around the base of this hill until it succeeds in joining the two sections. The dispossessed river now flows through a tunnel. Electric cars with whirring and clanging noises bowl along with modern indifference upon this grave of a torrent of the hills.

The motive of this main street is purely cosmopolitan. It undoubtedly typifies the United States better than does any existing thoroughfare, for it resembles the North and the South, the East and the West. For a moment a row of little wooden stores will look exactly like a portion of a small prairie village, but, later, one is confronted by a group of austere business blocks that are completely Eastern in expression. The street is bright at times with gaudy gypsy coloring; it is grey in places with dull and Puritanical hues. It is wealthy and poor; it is impertinent and courteous. It apparently comprehends all men and all moods and has little to say of itself. It is satisfied to exist without being defined nor classified.

And upon the pavement the crowd displays the reason of the street's knowledge of localities. There will be mingled an accent from the South, a hat and pair of boots from the West, a hurry and important engagement from the North, and a fine gown from the East.

An advantage of this condition is that no man need feel strange here. He may assure himself that there are men of his kind present. If, however, he is mistaken and there are no men of his kind in Hot Springs, he can conclude that he is a natural phenomenon and doomed to the curiosity of all peoples.

In Broadway perhaps people would run after a Turk to stare at his large extravagent trousers. Here it is doubtful if he would excite them at all. They would expect a Turk; they would comprehend that there were Turks and why there were Turks; they would accept the Turk with a mere raise of the eyebrows. This street thoroughly understands geography, and its experience of men is great. The instructors have been New York swells, Texas cattlemen, Denver mining kings, Chicago business men, and commercial travellers from the universe. This profound education has destroyed its curiosity and created a sort of a wide sympathy, not tender, but tolerant.

It is this absence of localism and the bigotry of classes which imparts to the entire town a peculiarly interesting flavor. There has been too general a contribution to admit two identical patterns. They were all different. And from these the town and the people were builded. Some of the hotels are enormous and like palaces. Some are like farm houses. Some are as small and plain as pine shanties. This superior education has impressed upon the town the fact that pocketbooks differentiate as do the distances to stars.

The bath houses for the most part stand in one row. They are close together and resemble mansions. They seem to be the abodes of peculiarly subdued and home-loving millionaires. The medicinal water is distributed under the supervision of the United States government, which in fact has reserved all the land save that valley in which the town lies. The water is first collected from all the springs into a principal reservoir. From thence it is again pumped through pipes to the bath houses. The government itself operates a free bath house, where 900 people bathe daily. The private ones charge a fee, which ranges from 20 to 60 cents.

Crowds swarm to these baths. A man becomes a creature of three conditions. He is about to take a bath—he is taking a bath—he has taken a bath. Invalids hobble slowly from their hotels, assisted perhaps by a pair of attendants. Soldiers from the U.S. Army and Navy Hospital trudge along assisting their rheumatic limbs with canes. All day there is a general and widespread march upon the baths.

In the quiet and intensely hot interiors of these buildings men involved in enormous bath-robes lounge in great rocking chairs. In other rooms the negro attendants scramble at the bidding of the bathers. Through the high windows the sunlight enters and pierces the curling masses of vapor which rise slowly in the heavy air.

There is naturally an Indian legend attached to these springs. In short, the Kanawagas were a great tribe with many hunters and warriors among them. They swung ponderous clubs with which they handily brained the ambitious but weaker warriors of other tribes. But at last a terrible scourge broke forth, and they, who had strode so proudly under the trees, crawled piteously on the pine-needles and called in beseeching voices toward the yellow sunset. After festivals, rites, avowals, sacrifices, the Spirit of the Wind heard the low clamor of his Indians and suddenly vapors began to emerge from the waters of what had been a cool mountain spring. The pool had turned hot. The wise men debated. At last, a courageous and inquisitive red man bathed. He liked it; others bathed. The scourge fled.

The servants at Hot Springs are usually that class of colored boys who come from the far South. They are very black and have good-humored, rolling eyes. They are not so sublime as Pullman-car porters. They have not that profound dignity, that impressive aspect of exhaustive learning, that inspiring independence, which the public admires in the other class. They are good-natured and not blessed with the sophistication that one can see at a distance. As waiters, they bend and slide and amble with consummate willingness. Sometimes they move at a little jig-trot.

And, in conclusion, there is a certain fervor, a certain intenseness about life in Hot Springs that reminds philosophers of the times when the Monmouth Park Racing Association and Phil Daly vied with each other in making Long Branch a beloved and celebrated city. It is not obvious, it is for the most part invisible, soundless. And yet it is to be discovered.

The traveller for the hat firm in Ogallala, Neb., remarked that a terrible storm had raged through the country during the second week in February. He surmised that it was the worst blizzard for many years. In New Orleans, the hackmen raised their fare to ten dollars, he had heard.

The youthful stranger, with the blonde and innocent hair, agreed with these remarks.

"Well," said the traveller for the hat firm, at last, "let's get a drink of that What-you-may-call-it Spring water, and then go and listen to the orchestra at the Arlington."

In the saloon, a man was leaning against the bar. As the traveller and the youthful stranger entered, this man said to the bar-tender: "I'll shake you for the drinks?"

"Same old game," said the traveller. "Always trying to beat the bar-tender, eh?"

"Well, I'll shake you for the drinks? How's that suit you?" said the man, ruffling his whiskers.

"All right," said the traveller for the hat firm in Ogallala, Neb. "I tell you what I'll do—I'll shake you for a dollar even."

"All right," said the man.

The traveller won. "Well, I tell you. I'll give you a chance to get your money back. I'll shake you for two bones."

The traveller won. "I'll shake you for four bones."

The traveller won.

"Got change for a five? I want a dollar back," said the man.

"No," said the traveller. "But I've got another five. I'll shake you for the two fives."

When the traveller for the hat firm in Ogallala, Neb., had won fifty dollars from the man with ruffled whiskers, the latter said: "Excuse me for a moment, please. You wait here for me, please. You're a winner."

As the man vanished, the traveller for the hat firm in Ogallala, Neb., turned to the youthful stranger, with the blonde and innocent hair, in an outburst of gleeful victory. "Well, that was easy," he cried ecstatically. "Fifty dollars in 'bout four minutes. Here— you take half and I'll take half, and we'll go blow it." He tendered five five-dollars to the youthful stranger with the blonde and innocent hair. The bar-tender was sleepily regardant. At the end of the bar was lounging a man with no drink in front of him.

The youthful stranger said: "Oh, you might as well keep it. I don't need it. I—"

"But, look here," exclaimed the traveller for the hat firm in Ogallala, Neb. "You might as well take it. I'd expect you to do the same if you won. It ain't anything among sporting men. You take half and I'll take half, and we'll go blow it. You're as welcome as sunrise, my dear fellow. Take it along—it's nothing. What are you kickin' about?" He spoke in tones of supreme anguish at this harsh treatment from a friend.

"No," said the youthful stranger, with the blonde and innocent hair, to the traveller for the hat firm in Ogallala, Neb., "I guess I'll stroll back up-town. I want to write a letter to my mother."

In the back room of the saloon, the man with the ruffled beard was silently picking hieroglyphics out of his whiskers.

3. Grand Opera in New Orleans

New Orleans, La., March 23.—
In the heart of the French quarter, there uprears a building that has the closest identification with the life of New Orleans. One of the first local prides of the citizens of this city is the French Opera House and its traditions of Parisian prime donne, its legends of ovations to famous tenors, all its memories of musical glory, which with its deeply scarred and worn exterior give it the dignity and the solemnity of a volume of history.

The approach to the opera house is through those quaint and narrow streets which are in themselves so graphic of tradition. Then suddenly appears among the low roofs a taller edifice, grey and white and leaden with age. The pillars of the portico align the outer curb of the sidewalk.

In the evening the little street before the building is gay with people. The electric light at the corner chooses its own time for illumination and takes occasional sputtering vacations. The diverging streets, too, present, for the most part, the assassin-like gloom of some European cities. But under the old portico there is a wealth of light, and the blithe and joyous clatter of many tongues. In the yel-

---

GRAND OPERA | IN NEW ORLEANS | [rule] | Music With a History of |More Than 100 Years. | [rule] | A MOST UNIQUE COMPANY | [rule] |The Only City in the Country That | Supports a Continual and Elaborate Production of |Grand Opera. | [rule] | (Copyright, 1895, by Bacheller, Johnson | & Bacheller.)

low rays from the adjacent cafes, move innumerable figures.

Grand opera in New Orleans has a history of a hundred years. Davis, a French refugee from San Domingo, came here in 1790, and, with the true spirit of his nation, it was no trouble at all for him to change at once from a participant in the bloody scuffling at San Domingo to a conductor of grand opera. In 1814, the Orleans theatre was built at the corner of Orleans and Bourbon streets. Madame Devries was singing the role of Fides in "The Prophet" at this theatre when she conceived the idea of naming her daughter after the title of her part, and this sudden inspiration is responsible for the name of the present famous Parisian singer. Mme. Witman, Mme. Colson, M. Du Luc, M. De La Grave, M. Le Croix, M. Crambade and M. Jenibrel were all imported from Paris to this house to satisfy the vast enthusiasm of the French New Orleans public.

This house was the heart of the social life of the city. All the existence of the old Creole aristocracy was centered in the opera. The spirited and earnest gentlemen of the day exchanged cards with a magnificent frequence in this building. In fact, it is said that more duels were arranged there than in any other building in the world. And a certain great feature were the "loges grilles"—latticed boxes—where families in mourning could listen to the opera without being observed by the spectators.

In 1859, the present opera house was erected. The Orleans had become too small. Gradually, the opera had acquired a patronage that comprised the wealthy classes of both the French and American populations, as well as the masses of the people. Mathieu and Tournier were the two tenors who, at this time, soared to brilliant heights of popularity. Adelina Patti was the star of 1860. This was before she began her farewell tours; in fact, it was her American debut. Singer appeared in 1881, Gerster in 1882, De Murska in 1885, Martinez in 1889. There are, of course, veterans in open attendance who love to tell of the memorable events of the past, and their favorite theme is of the time when Devoyod, the famous baritone, was fairly overwhelmed at his benefit in 1874, with flowers, kisses, jewelry, devotion, adoration. Men stood on each other's backs in the parquet and the management was obliged to remove the negroes out of the fourth tier in order to make room.

New Orleans is the only city in the United States that supports a continual and elaborate production of grand opera. And, as mentioned, New Orleans has done so for quite a hundred years. In New York it is, perhaps, always something of a venture. From time to time a manager acquires sufficient courage. He speculates long and deeply, and then afterward he wears the pious air of a man who has dared everything for the sake of a beloved art. And he is altogether entitled to wear this air of piety.

Here the opera is supported by the entire populance. The lights of the company are the deities of the masses. Their adherents wrangle over their merits. There is a vast and elemental interest and enthusiasm.

Above all, the prices are arranged so that building sites do not have to be exchanged for tickets. As a matter of fact, the opera can be seen for ten cents. The best seats in the house are purchased for one dollar and fifty cents. This does not make a taste for grand opera to be thorns in the flesh of a small vendor of olives or matches.

Perhaps these things adjust themselves. It may be that it is only when a public attains the cultivation of a New Orleans public that cheap opera can be given it. Perhaps it is necessary to charge a man the price of a schooner yacht in order to instruct him.

The company this year is headed by Madame Laville. She is a soprano who sings with a dramatic comprehension that is unusual. She renders the principal roles in all the weightier operas given, with an impressive emotional sincerity. Her fine voice and her artistic earnestness have caused her to be immensely popular. Anasty, the tenor, and Chavaroche, the basso, are usually associated with her in the productions.

The chorus is a commendable portion of the company. There is a distinct dash and vigor in their singing and acting which is not always observed in chorus. This air of spirit is more apparent in the male part of the chorus than in the female. For example, in the first act of "La Juive" there is a little terse quarrel of peasants, enduring just a few seconds, which the men of the chorus render with a sudden snap and intensity which is evidently impossible to the usual chorus men who conduct the same little vignette with the fire and fervor of a row of box-wood plants.

In all their appearances, they are in earnest, engrossed in the opera.

The orchestra is an organization of eighty pieces. The leadership is perfectly capable and wise, and the orchestra plays well, animated by the single purpose of creating artistic earnest, engrossed in the opera.

The company often varies its grand opera with little interjections of light opera. Its public depends almost entirely upon it for amusement as well as for musical thought. There are stars enough to give three or four operas at one time and the chorus is versatile.

In "Les Amours du Diable," "Les Dragons de Villars," "Madame Angot," and operas of this class, the principal role is usually sung by Madame St. Laurent.

And this is another quite strange fact concerning localism of the opera company. Madame St. Laurent, it may be said, is absolutely unknown to the country at large. She is not supposed to regret it, since her audience here appreciates her in that proprietary way of people who are fellow-countrymen, but it seems wonderful that such a marvelously clever woman's fame for finesse and skill on the beloved comic opera boards should go no farther than the limits of this city, when as a matter of truth there are so many of the world's exalted in light comic opera careers who could gain much instruction by a series of attendances at Madame St. Laurent's school.

At present, the company is existing in a state that ordinarily devours an operatic company in two days. In short it is without a manager. However, the performances continue and there has been no sign yet of the usual ear-splitting row. The company is managing itself. It must be said again that this is the unique opera company of the world.

When the great question of grand opera is agitated in other cities, people can look toward New Orleans and see certain incredible things. They can see grand opera that is an institution of a century. They can see grand opera given at cheap prices and they can see grand opera patronized by all classes.

4. The Fête of Mardi Gras

It rained toward the latter part of the week and the visitors who had already arrived began to shake their heads as they proceeded carefully over the thin coating of black mud that lay upon the uneven stones of the streets. The citizens, however, remained in serene and unshaken faith. No, it would not rain on Mardi Gras. It never rained then. There would be fine weather—just wait.

And, in truth, when Sunday appeared it was of the quality of spring, fair, soft and balmy with the singularly lucid atmosphere of the southland. On Canal street swarmed an expectant crowd dodging in and about the upright joists that had been placed to support the balconies. The windows of the hotels and clubs were filled with visitors from other cities taking a preliminary view of the wide street with its masses of people upon the side-walks and upon the strip of yellow grass in the middle of the avenue where, too, at short intervals ran mule cars and electric cars and the cars of a stream tramway proceeding slowly through the throng and filling the air with the clamor of gongs. In the breeze that came over the housetops, decorations of purple and green and gold gently fluttered.

At noon on Monday the throng occupying the avenue had been largely augmented. People turned their eyes toward the levee where, because the waters of the river could in no wise be seen, the avenue seemed to be projected into the air. In the steel-colored sky some black smoke drifted upward. Then at last the masts and two tan stacks of a steamer moved slowly into view, afar off, over the multitude of heads in the street. Later there could be seen the glit-

---

THE FÊTE OF MARDI GRAS. | [rule] | Stephen Crane Describes the Celebration of | This Remarkable Festival | [rule] | VERY HIGH JINKS IN NEW ORLEANS | [rule] | The Extraordinary Pageant With | Its Display of Color and [word illegible] | —The Main Show and the | Side Shows. | [rule] |(Copyright 1896, by Bacheller, Johnson & Bacheller.)

ter of many approaching bayonets and the steady beat of martial music. The crowds on the sidewalk underwent an anticipatory convulsion. Rex, his majesty of the carnival time, had come. There was a sudden interpolation of crimson color into the black masses of people down the avenue.

All Tuesday morning, the usual sombre clothes of citizens in the street were brightened by the gypsy hues of the maskers. Small boys arrayed in wondrous garments to represent monkeys, gnomes, imps, parrots, anything but small boys, paraded in bands and reaped a deep delight when they found a victim for their skill in badinage. And much older boys, temporarily represented as all manner of nondescript personages, rambled over the city in the full joy of being at their own devices with a sort of mild license to caper and crack jokes into the air. At noon, Canal street was a river of human bodies moving slowly. At dusk, it was a sea, in which contrary currents indolently opposed each other. The fronts of the clubs and principal buildings suddenly became outlined in the shine of electric lights and, in these brilliant frames, symbolistic initials appeared. The royal colors of green and purple and gold shone forth in bunting and silk and glass. Between a curb and one of the horse car tracks a deep row of people had collected and the small street-cars came along at regular and monotonous intervals and scraped some of them away. The boxes and stands had already begun to fill up and the people in them turned their faces toward the darkness of the end of the street. In one of the stands was a space reserved for his majesty, Rex, his queen and court. From these stands, the avenue resembled a vast black sea save where here and there gleamed the costumes of a group of maskers or where a street-car fought its irritatingly painful way through the throng.

Ultimately, the king, gorgeous in his royal robes and his jewels, and with his features behind a huge Cossack beard, came slowly down the sloping stand with his queen, and followed by his glittering court. Instantly this vast black expanse of the street became an ocean of faces, a great stretch of eager human countenances in which the eyes—rolled slowly. A hoarse rumble of voices arose;

then, later, a shout as if a rocket had been seen to ascend. "A-a-ah!"

Then the patient crowd settled into a profound and silent contemplation of their carnival ruler. Occasionally a man stretched forth his neck to peer down the street for the procession and frequently maskers engaged in a tumultuous frolic. Too, as mentioned, the street-cars scraped sightseers from the curbs that bounded the grass plots in the middle of the street but, for the most part, this great mass of people remained silent, patient, motionless.

Suddenly a man shouted: "Here it comes!" Far over the heads could be seen a banner that caught a vivid reflection from some lights beneath it. At the side of the street, a negro coachman had crawled into the gloom of a corner of his victoria and gone to sleep. An agitated bystander yelled at him: "Come, uncle, wake up! They're comin' and they'll chase you away from here." The old man hastily drew on his shoes again and crawled up on his box. "Yas, I raiken dey is. Dey'll done bully me outa year an' I better had be gittin'." But this was not the procession at all but some marauding company of maskers. When he had gathered up his reins and turned for a last glance to the rear, the banner had vanished. He made a gesture of deep scorn at the man who had aroused him. "Aw! Aw! dat wan no percession—"

In the middle of the street some little boys had created a riot. They were dressed as some strange kind of white apes but the tails of their suits were so long and so neatly stuffed with cotton that the ends could be pulled around in front and used very effectively as clubs. With these weapons they had belabored some little boys who were exhibiting as minstrels, and an exciting combat had at once ensued between the minstrels and the apes.

Meanwhile, the street-cars had become blocked, and, standing thus in the middle of the wide streets, they made fine and cheap stands from which to view the procession as it passed to the right of them. Women with numerous children, old couples, and people without these reasons presented an interminable row of faces at the windows of an interminable row of cars.

Around the gleaming place where sat their majesties and the court, a throng in milder raiment, in which shone many white conventional shirt fronts, slowly gathered. Ladies with dainty gestures raised their lorgnettes to stare into the dark perspective of the avenue. The king lifted his sceptre and examined it with interest. The ladies of the court chatted, turning their heads from one to another, their eyes shining. With the vivid light upon this balcony, the scene of violet and white had all the distinctness of a marvelous painting. The procession was delayed. Some of the court seemed petulant. If the king was bored his weariness was hidden in his flowing beard.

Down in the democratic semi-gloom of the street stood a young girl, her hand upon the arm of a young man. This girl had remained for a long time motionless, her eyes raised at an angle and fixed upon the queen. Her lips were a little way parted, her cheeks were subtly flushed. And into this glance there was a profundity of awe, admiration. She dreamed, and this dream was so splendid, so full of rainbow glories, that even the scene before her was merely a guide. The dream was broken by a negro teamster who came through the crowd with three mules and a dray. He had become so ferocious toward a small boy who had dived between the lead mule and the wheel team that he could not have the ordinary care for people's safety. A large section of crowd had to scurry. There was some eloquent abuse.

Meanwhile the king, inscrutable behind his beard, looked down at his subjects. The queen, regal alike in fact and carnival, talked to her ladies. And turned always toward the royal pair was this waxen sea of faces. Above the arcs and squares of illumination hung a sky like black velvet.

Down the avenue there appeared a pale purple haze. Presently the forms of mounted policemen could be seen outlined in it. A rocket went slantingly upward. There was some mild and good-natured jostling. A voice cried out: "Ah, git off de eart' an' give de grass a chanct t' grow." A man with the shaven face and mobile lips of an actor immediately said: "Great Scott! I know that breed! What's he doing away down here?"

The strains of a march came plainly. The haze grew brighter and varied its color. In the background could be seen the form of one of the floats, but in the incoherent shadows it resembled a striding giant. A row of negro babies in their eagerness peered out too far and toppled from the curb. The gutter contained about two inches of water.

The solitary mounted policeman who formed the extreme advance guard was gaily assaulted by an Indian chief, a pirate, and some apes. His horse reared and plunged and he wrenched his arm free of them. He rode on laughing good naturedly. After him came others, insistent and perfectly serious in their business of clearing the street, but apparently always good natured and civil.

After the police, the procession slowly came through between the two black lines of people. From the high stands it resembled a long monster of golden fire upon which gleamed frequently dazzling spots of purple and green. The glittering floats creaked slowly over the stones and the shining and enormous emblems in wood and paper and cloth gently vibrated with a persistent and endless motion. The luminous figures upon them hung on with one hand while they waved the other gaily at the crowd.

The floats looked in the distance like vast confections. Some were of a fine cool green, like spring water seen in the sun-light, while others were of the hue of violets. These soft colors imparted to the great moving masses a fairy-like quality as if a wind might blow them, light and unresisting, high into the sky. In long lines at either side marched negroes in blood-red gnome cloaks, bearing torches with reflectors, which shed a strong and continual orange glare upon the floats. And, dragging slowly at the traces, the mules too were hidden in red cloaks, although occasionally a thoughtful and indifferent countenance appeared, and upon it an expression of deep and far-away reflection. Girls leaned over balconies and shouted: "Ah, there's Comus! There he is! Comus, Comus, look this way!"

This night's prince, high in air and crowned, gestured and bowed amiably at the cheers. One found one's self staring at the mask and wondering, not of the features, but of the emotion, and feeling exasperated at the baffling cover.

Further down the gorgeous line the float of the great god Pan started from a halt with a sudden jerk and almost precipitated him from his high estate.

A masker in red and green expressed in pantomime from his perch on a float his great anxiety to present a certain box tied with ribbons to some young men in the street. The young men yelled: "Yes! Go ahead! Let'er come." The masker threw the box swiftly; the astonished young men dodged. But the masker had a string to it and it returned to his hand. A derisive howl came from the crowd. As the float moved on, the masker gestured mockingly. It seemed wonderful in some way that throughout this incident that mask should remain imperturbable, unchanged, with the same expression of extraordinary ferocity with which it had been created.

Vivid fires of red, yellow, purple, white, sputtered forth their luminous smoke. Bands clashed interminably. And because of the glare of light the faces of the crowd became pallid and, in the immobility of expression, death-like, save for the eyes which glinted with delight.

In the balconies near the king and queen, ladies leaned forward intently. Upon the floats, the glittering maskers turned at once toward this array of silent, deeply observant women. The display here found itself out-displayed. And the occasional, the temporary royalties gazed at the eternal royalty of beautiful women. Occasionally from these high stands, a gloved hand lifted a handkerchief and waved it.

As soon as the procession had passed, the crowd swirled in one mass over the avenue as the waters close after the passage of a vessel.

Down in the French quarter, the narrow and gloomy street that leads to the famous opera house suddenly achieved all the radiance of light and splendor of hue which had illuminated Canal street. From the profoundly dark side streets the procession, as it passed the corners, bore the appearance of a wide and shining frieze upon which were painted marvelous moving figures in violet, gold, light green. In front of the solemn pillars of the opera house each float was suddenly made a bare splendor, as its imps, its knights and its flower girls clambered hastily down. Later, the tiny glow of carriage lamps was seen up the street. Their majesties were coming to their grand ball.

In other gloomy streets, the negroes, still in their blood-red gnome cloaks, could be seen urging the mules in front of the deserted floats which gleamed like frost in the darkness.

5. Galveston, Texas, in 1895

It is the fortune of travellers to take note of differences and publish them to their friends. It is the differences that are supposed to be valuable. The travellers seek them bravely, and cudgel their wits to find means to unearth them. But in this search they are confronted continually by the resemblances; and the intrusion of commonplace and most obvious similarity into a field that is being ploughed in the romantic fashion is what causes an occasional resort to the imagination.

The winter found a cowboy in south-western Nebraska who had just ended a journey from Kansas City, and he swore bitterly as he remembered how little boys in Kansas City followed him about in order to contemplate his wide-brimmed hat. His vivid description of this incident would have been instructive to many Eastern readers. The fact that little boys in Kansas City could be profoundly interested in the sight of a wide-hatted cowboy would amaze a certain proportion of the populace. Where then can one expect cowboys if not in Kansas City? As a matter of truth, however, a steam boiler with four legs and a tail, galloping down the main street of the town, would create no more enthusiasm there than a real cow-

GALVESTON, TEXAS, IN 1895. BY|THE LATE STEPHEN CRANE.

puncher. For years the farmers have been driving the cattlemen back, back toward the mountains and into Kansas, and Nebraska has come to an almost universal condition of yellow trolly-cars with clanging gongs and whirring wheels, and conductors who don't give a curse for the public. And travellers tumbling over each other in their haste to trumpet the radical differences between Eastern and Western life have created a generally wrong opinion. No one has yet dared to declare that if a man drew three treys to Syracuse, N.Y., in many a Western city, the man would be blessed with a full house. The declaration has no commercial value. There is a distinct fascination in being aware that in some parts of the world there are purple pigs, and children who are born with china mugs dangling where their ears should be. It is this fact which makes men sometimes grab tradition in wonder; color and attach contemporaneous date-lines to it. It is this fact which has kept the sweeping march of the West from being chronicled in any particularly true manner.

In a word, it is the passion for differences which has prevented a general knowledge of the resemblances.

If a man comes to Galveston resolved to discover every curious thing possible, and to display every point where Galveston differed from other parts of the universe, he would have the usual difficulty in shutting his eyes to the similarities. Galveston is often original, full of distinctive characters. But it is not like a town in the moon. There are, of course, a thousand details of street color and life which are thoroughly typical of any American city. The square brick business blocks, the mazes of telegraph wires, the trolly-cars clamoring up and down the streets, the passing crowd, the slight fringe of reflective and reposeful men on the curb, all disappoint the traveller, and he goes out in the sand somewhere and digs in order to learn if all Galveston clams are not schooner-rigged.

Accounts of these variations are quaint and interesting reading, to be sure, but then, after all, there are the great and elemental facts of American life. The cities differ as peas—in complexion, in size, in temperature—but the fundamental part, the composition, remains.

There has been a wide education in distinctions. It might be furtively suggested that the American people did not thoroughly know their mighty kinship, their universal emotions, their identical view-points upon many matters about which little is said. Of course, when the foreign element is injected very strongly, a town becomes strange, unfathomable, wearing a sort of guilty air which puzzles the American eye. There begins then a great diversity, and peas become turnips, and the differences are profound. With them, however, this prelude has nothing to do. It is a mere attempt to impress a reader with the importance of remembering that an illustration of Galveston streets can easily be obtained in Maine. Also, that the Gulf of Mexico could be mistaken for the Atlantic Ocean, and that its name is not printed upon it in tall red letters, notwithstanding the legend which has been supported by the geographies.

There are but three lifts in the buildings of Galveston. This is not because the people are skilled climbers; it is because the buildings are for the most part not high.

A certain Colonel Menard bought this end of the island of Galveston from the Republic of Texas in 1838 for fifty thousand dollars. He had a premonition of the value of wide streets for the city of his dreams, and he established a minimum width of seventy feet. The widest of the avenues is one hundred and fifty feet. The fact that this is not extraordinary for 1898 does not prevent it from being marvellous as municipal forethought in 1838.

In 1874 the United States Government decided to erect stone jetties at the entrance to the harbor of Galveston in order to deepen the water on the outer and inner bars, whose shallowness compelled deep-water ships to remain outside and use lighters to transfer their cargoes to the wharves of the city. Work on the jetties was in progress when I was in Galveston in 1895—in fact, two long, low black fingers of stone stretched into the Gulf. There are men still living who had confidence in the Governmental decision of 1874, and these men now point with pride to the jetties and say that the United States Government is nothing if not inevitable.

The soundings at mean low tide were thirteen feet on the inner bar and about twelve feet on the outer bar. At present there is twenty-three feet of water where once was the inner bar, and as the jetties have crept toward the sea they have achieved eighteen feet of water in the channel of the outer bar at mean low tide. The plan is to gain a depth of thirty feet. The cost is to be about seven million dollars.

Undoubtedly in 1874 the people of Galveston celebrated the decision of the Government with great applause, and prepared to welcome mammoth steamers at the wharves during the next spring. It was in 1889, however, that matters took conclusive form. In 1895 the prayer of Galveston materalised.

In 1889, Iowa, Nebraska, Missouri, Kansas, California, Arkansas, Texas, Wyoming, and New Mexico began a serious pursuit of Congress. Certain products of these States and Territories could not be exported with profit, owing to the high rate for transportation to eastern ports. They demanded a harbor on the coast of Texas with a depth and area sufficient for great sea-crossing steamers. The board of army engineers which was appointed by Congress decided on Galveston as the point. The plan was to obtain by means of artificial constructions a volume and velocity of tidal flow that would maintain a navigable channel. The jetties are seven thousand feet apart, in order to allow ample room for the escape of the enormous flow of water from the inner bar.

Galveston has always been substantial and undeviating in its amount of business. Soon after the war it attained a commercial solidity, and its progress has been steady but quite slow. The citizens now, however, are lying in wait for a real Western boom. Those products of the West which have been walled in by the railroad transportation rates to eastern ports are now expected to pass through Galveston. An air of hope pervades the countenance of each business man. The city, however, exported 1,500,000 bales of cotton last season, and the Chamber of Commerce has already celebrated the fact.

A train approaches the Island of Galveston by means of a long steel bridge across a bay, which glitters like burnished metal in the winter-time sunlight. The vast number of white two-storied frame houses in the outskirts would remind one of New England, if it were not that the island is level as a floor. Later, in the commercial part of the town, appear the conventional business houses and the trolly-cars. Far up the cross-streets is the faint upheaval of the surf of the breeze-blown Gulf, and in the other direction the cotton steamers are arrayed with a fresco upon their black sides of dusky chuckling stevedores handling the huge bales amid a continual and foreign conversation, in which all the subtle and incomprehensible gossip of their social relations goes from mouth to mouth, the bales leaving little tufts of cotton all over their clothing.

Galveston has a rather extraordinary number of very wealthy people. Along the finely-paved drives their residences can be seen, modern for the most part and poor in architecture. Occasionally, however, one comes upon a typical Southern mansion, its galleries giving it a solemn shade and its whole air one of fine and enduring dignity. The palms standing in the grounds of these houses seem to pause at this time of year, and patiently abide the coming of the hot breath of summer. They still remain of a steadfast green and their color is a wine.

Underfoot the grass is of a yellow hue, here and there patched with a faint impending verdancy. The famous snowstorm here this winter played havoc with the color of the vegetation, and one can now observe the gradual recovery of the trees, the shrubbery, the grass. In this vivid sunlight their vitality becomes enormous.

This storm also had a great effect upon the minds of the citizens. They would not have been more astonished if it had rained suspender buttons. The writer read descriptions of this storm in the newspapers of the date. Since his arrival here he has listened to 574 accounts of it.

Galveston has the aspect of a seaport. New York is not a seaport; a seaport is, however, a certain detail of New York. But in Galveston the docks, the ships, the sailors, are a large element in the life of the town. Also, one can sometimes find here that marvelous type, the American sailor. American seamen are not numerous enough to ever depreciate in value. A town that can produce a copy of the American sailor should encase him in bronze and unveil him on the Fourth of July. A veteran of the waves explained to the writer the reason that American youths do not go to sea. He said it was because saddles are too expensive. The writer congratulated the veteran of the waves upon his lucid explanation of this great question.

Galveston has its own summer resorts. In the heat of the season, life becomes sluggish in the streets. Men move about with an extraordinary caution as if they expected to be shot as they approached each corner.

At the beach, however, there is a large hotel which overflows with humanity, and in front is, perhaps, the most comfortable structure in the way of bath-houses known to the race. Many of the rooms are ranged about the foot of a large dome. A gallery connects them, but the principal floor to this structure is the sea itself, to which a flight of steps leads. Galveston's 35,000 people divide among themselves in summer a reliable wind from the Gulf.

There is a distinctly cosmopolitan character to Galveston's people. There are men from everywhere. The city does not represent Texas. It is unmistakably American, but in a general manner. Certain Texas differentiations are not observable in this city.

Withal, the people have the Southern frankness, the honesty which enables them to meet a stranger without deep suspicion, and they are the masters of a hospitality which is instructive to cynics.

6. Patriot Shrine of Texas

San Antonio, Tex., Jan. 6.—
"Ah," they said, "you are going to San Anton? I wish I was. There's a town for you!"

PATRIOT SHRINE OF TEXAS | [rule] | Stephen Crane's Impressions of San Antonio | and the Alamo | [rule] | Evidence of a Northern Invasion | [rule] | Derby Hats and Trolley Cars Disturb | an Atmosphere of Romance—How | Bowie and Crockett Met | Santa Ana

From all manner of people, business men, consumptive men, curious men and wealthy men, there came an exhibition of a profound affection for San Antonio. It seemed to symbolize for them the poetry of life in Texas.

There is an eloquent description of the city which makes it consist of three old ruins and a row of Mexicans sitting in the sun. The author, of course, visited San Antonio in the year 1101. While this is undoubtedly a masterly literary effect, one can feel glad that after all we don't steer our ships according to these literary effects.

At first the city presents a totally modern aspect to the astonished visitor. The principal streets are lanes between rows of handsome business blocks and upon them proceeds with important uproar the terrible and almighty trolley car. The prevailing type of citizen is not seated in the sun; on the contrary he is making his way with the speed and intentness of one who competes in a community that is commercially in earnest. And the victorious derby hat of the north spreads its wings in the holy place of legends.

This is the dominant quality. This is the principal color of San Antonio. Later one begins to see that these edifices of stone and brick and iron are reared on ashes, upon the amitions of a race. It expresses again the victory of the north. The serene Anglo-Saxon erects business blocks upon the dreams of transient monks; he strings telegraph wires across the face of their sky of hope and over the energy, the efforts, the accomplishments of these pious fathers of the early church passes the wheel, the hoof, the heel.

Here and there, however, one finds in the main part of the town little old buildings yellow with age, solemn and severe in outline, that have escaped by a miracle or by a historical importance the whirl of the modern life. In the Mexican quarters there remains, too, much of the old character, but despite the tenderness which San Antonio feels for these monuments, the unprotected mass of them must get trampled into shapeless dust which lies always behind the march of this terrible century. The feet of the years will go through many old roofs.

Trolley cars are merciless animals. They gorge themselves with relics. They make really coherent history too like an omelet. If a trolley car had trolleyed around Jericho, the city would not have fallen; it would have exploded.

Centuries ago the white and gold banner of Spain came up out of the sea and the Indians, mere dots of black on the vast Texan plain, saw a moving glitter of silver warriors on the horizon's edge. There came then the long battle of soldier and priest, side by side, against these stubborn barbaric hordes, who wished to retain both their gods and their lands. Sword and crozier made frenzied circles in the air. The soldiers varied their fights with the Indians by fighting the French, and both the Indians and the French occasionally polished their armor for them with great neatness and skill.

During the interval of peace and interval of war, toiled the pious monks, erecting missions, digging ditches, making farms and cudgeling their Indians in and out of the church. Sometimes, when the venerable fathers ran short of Indians to convert the soldiers went on expeditions and returned dragging a few score. The settlement prospered. Upon the gently rolling plains the mission churches with their yellow stone towers outlined upon the sky called with their bells at evening a multitude of friars and meek Indians and gleaming soldiers to service in the shadows before the flaming candles, the solemn shrine, the slow-pacing, chanting priests. And wicked and hopeless Indians, hearing these bells, scudded off into the blue twilight of the prairie.

The ruins of these missions are now besieged in the valley south of the city by indomitable thickets of mesquite. They rear their battered heads, their soundless towers, over dead forms, the graves of monks; and of the Spanish soldiers not one so much as flourishes a dagger.

Time has torn at these pale yellow structures and overturned walls and towers here and there, defaced this and obliterated that. Relic hunters with their singular rapacity have dragged down little saints from their niches and pulled important stones from arches. They have performed offices of destruction of which the wind and the rain of the innumerable years was not capable. They are part of the general scheme of attack by nature.

The wind blows because it is the wind, the rain beats because it is the rain, the relic hunters hunt because they are relic hunters. Who can fathom the ways of nature? She thrusts her spear in the eye of Tradition and her agents feed on his locks. A little guide book published here contains one of these "Good friend, forbear—" orations. But still this desperate massacre of the beautiful carvings goes on and it would take the ghosts of the monks with the ghosts of scourges, the phantoms of soldiers with the phantoms of swords, a scowling, spectral party, to stop the destruction. In the meantime these portentous monuments to the toil, the profound convictions of the fathers, remain stolid and unyielding, with the bravery of stone, until it appears like the last stand of an army. Many years will charge them before the courage will abate which was injected into the mortar by the skillful monks.

It is something of a habit among the newspaper men and others who write here to say: "Well, there's a good market for Alamo stuff, now!" Or perhaps they say: "Too bad! Alamo stuff isn't going very strong, now." Literary aspirants of the locality, as soon as they finish writing about Her Eyes, begin on the Alamo. Statistics show that 69,710 writers have begun at the Alamo.

Notwithstanding this fact, the Alamo remains the greatest memorial to courage which civilization has allowed to stand. The quaint and curious little building fronts on one of the most popular plazas of the city and because of Travis, Crockett, Bowie and their comrades it maintains dignity amid the taller, modern structures which front it. It is the tomb of the fiery emotions of Texans who refused to admit that numbers and Mexicans were arguments. Whether the swirl of life, the crowd upon the streets, pauses to look or not, the spirit that lives in this building, its air of contemplative silence, is as eloquent as an old battle flag.

The first Americans to visit San Antonio arrived in irons. This was the year 1800. There were eleven of them. They had fought 150 Spanish soldiers on the eastern frontier and, by one of those incomprehensible chances which so often decides the color of battles, they had lost the fight. Afterward, Americans began to filter down through Lousiana until in 1834 there were enough of them to openly disagree with the young federal government in the City of

Mexico, although there was not really any great number of them. Santa Ana didn't give a tin whistle for the people of Texas. He assured himself that he was capable of managing the republic of Mexico and after coming to this decision he said to himself that that part of it which formed the state of Texas had better remain quiet with the others. In writing of what followed, a Mexican sergeant says: "The Texans fought like devils."

There was a culmination at the old mission of the Alamo in 1836. This structure then consisted of a rectangular stone parapet 190 feet long and about 120 feet wide with the existing Church of the Alamo in the southeast corner. Colonel William B. Travis, David Crockett and Colonel Bowie, whose monument is a knife with a peculiar blade, were in this enclosure with a garrison of something like 150 men when they heard that Santa Ana was marching against them with an army of 4,000. The Texans shut themselves in the mission and when Santa Ana demanded their surrender they fired a cannon and inaugurated the most appalling conflict of the continent.

Once Colonel Travis called his men together during a lull of the battle and said to them: "Our fate is sealed. ° ° ° Our friends were evidently not informed of our perilous situation in time to save us. Doubtless they would have been here by this time if they had expected any considerable force of the enemy. ° ° ° Then we must die."

He pointed out to them the three ways of being killed—surrendering to the enemy and being executed, making a rush through the enemy's lines and getting shot before they could inflict much damage, or staying in the Alamo and holding out to the last, making themselves into a huge and terrible porcupine to be swallowed by the Mexican god of war. All the men save one adopted the last plan with their colonel.

This minority was a man named Rose. "I'm not prepared to die, and shall not do so if I can avoid it." He was some kind of a dogged philosopher. Perhaps he said: "What's the use?" There is a strange inverted courage in the manner in which he faced his companions with this sudden and short refusal in the midst of a general exhibition of supreme bravery. "No," he said. He bade them adieu and climbed the wall. Upon its top he turned to look down at the upturned faces of his silent comrades.

After the battle there were 521 dead Mexicans mingled with the corpses of the Texans.

The Mexicans form a certain large part of the population of San Antonio. Modern inventions have driven them toward the suburbs, but they are still seen upon the main streets in the ratio of one to eight and in their distant quarter of course they swarm. A small percentage have reached positions of business eminence.

The men wear for the most part wide-brimmed hats with peaked crowns, and under these shelters appear their brown faces and the inevitable cigarettes. The remainder of their apparel has become rather Americanized, but the hat of romance is still superior. Many of the young girls are pretty, and all of the old ones are ugly. These latter squat like clay images and the lines upon their faces, and especially about the eyes, make it appear as if they were always staring into the eye of a blinding sun.

Upon one of the plazas, Mexican vendors with open-air stands sell food that tastes exactly like pounded fire-brick from hades —Chili con carne, tamales, enchiladas, chili verde, frijoles. In the soft atmosphere of the southern night, the cheap glass bottles upon the stands shine like crystal and the lamps glow with a tender radiance. A hum of conversation ascends from the strolling visitors who are at their social shrine.

The prairie about San Antonio is wrinkled into long, low hills, like immense waves and upon them spreads a wilderness of the persistent mesquite, a bush that grows in defiance of everything. Some forty years ago the mesquite first assailed the prairies about the city and now from various high points it can be seen to extend to the joining to earth and sky. The individual bushes do not grow close together and roads and bridle paths cut through the dwarf forest in all directions. A certain class of Mexicans dwell in hovels amid the mesquite.

In the Mexican quarter of the town the gambling houses are crowded nightly and before the serene dealers lie little stacks of silver dollars. A Mexican may not be able to raise enough money to buy beef tea for his dying grandmother, but he can always stake himself for a game of monte.

Upon a hillock of the prairie in the outskirts of the city is situated the government military post, Fort Sam Houston. There are four beautiful yellow and blue squadrons of cavalry, two beautiful red and blue batteries of light artillery and six beautiful white and blue companies of infantry. Officers' row resembles a collection of Newport cottages. There are magnificent lawns and gardens. The presence of so many officers of the line beside the gorgeous members of the staff of the commanding general imparts a certain brilliant quality to San Antonio society. The drills upon the wide parade ground make a citizen proud.

7. Stephen Crane in Mexico: I

City of Mexico, July 4.—
The train rolled out of the Americanisms of San Antonio—the coal and lumber yards, the lines of freight cars, the innumerable tracks and black cinder paths—and into the southern expanses of mesquite.

In the smoking compartment, the capitalist from Chicago said to the archaeologist from Boston: "Well, here we go." The archaeologist smiled with placid joy.

The brown wilderness of mesquite drifted steadily and for hours

---

STEPHEN CRANE IN MEXICO. | [rule] | From San Antonio to the Ancient City of the | Aztecs. | [rule] | THROUGH CACTUS AND MES-QUITE. | [rule] | The Author of "The Black Riders" | Describes a Trip as Picturesque as | any to be Taken in America. | [rule] | (Copyright, 1895, Bacheller, Johnson & Bachel- | ler.)

past the car windows. Occasionally a little ranch appeared half-buried in the bushes.

In the door-yard of one some little calicoed babies were playing and in the door-way itself a woman stood leaning her head against the post of it and regarding the train listlessly. Pale, worn, dejected, in her old and soiled gown, she was of a type to be seen north, east, south, west.

"That'll be one of our best glimpses of American civilization," observed the archaeologist then.

Cactus plants spread their broad pulpy leaves on the soil of reddish brown in the shade of the mesquite bushes. A thin silvery vapor appeared at the horizon.

"Say, I met my first Mexican, day before yesterday," said the capitalist. "Coming over from New Orleans. He was a peach. He could really talk more of the English language than any man I've ever heard. He talked like a mill-wheel. He had the happy social faculty of making everybody intent upon his conversation. You couldn't help it, you know. He put every sentence in the form of a question. 'San Anton' fine town—uh? F-i-n-n-e—uh? Gude beesness there—uh? Yes gude place for beesness—uh?" We all had to keep saying 'yes,' or 'Certainly,' or 'you bet your life,' at intervals of about three seconds."

"I went to school with some Cubans up north when I was a boy," said the archaeologist, and they taught me to swear in Spanish. I'm all right in that. I can—"

"Don't you understand the conversational part at all?" demanded the capitalist.

"No," replied the archaeologist.

"Got friends in the City of Mexico?"

"No!"

"Well, by jiminy, you're going going to have a daisy time!"

"Why, do you speak the language?"

"No!"

"Got any friends in the city?"

"No!"

"Thunder!"

These mutual acknowledgements riveted the two men together. In this invasion, in which they were both facing the unknown, an acquaintance was a prize.

As the train went on over the astonishing brown sea of mesquite, there began to appear little prophecies of Mexico. A Mexican woman, perhaps, crouched in the door of a hut, her bare arms folded, her knees almost touching her chin, her head leaned against the door-post. Or perhaps a dusky sheep-herder in peaked sombrero and clothes the color of tan-bark standing beside the track, his inscrutable visage turned toward the train. A cloud of white dust rising above the dull-colored bushes denoted the position of his flock. Over this lonely wilderness vast silence hung, a speckless sky, ignorant of bird or cloud.

"Look at this," said the capitalist.

"Look at that," said the archaeologist.

These premonitory signs threw them into fever of anticipation. "Say, how much longer before we get to Laredo?" The conductor grinned. He recognized some usual, some typical aspect in this impatience. "Oh, a long time yet."

But then, finally, when the whole prairie had turned a faint preparatory shadow-blue, someone told them: "See those low hills off yonder? Well, they're beyond the Rio Grande."

"Get out—are they?"

A sheep-herder with his flock raising pale dust-clouds over the lonely mesquite could no longer interest them. Their eyes were fastened on the low hills beyond the Rio Grande.

"There it is! There's the river!"

"Ah, no, it ain't!"

"I say it is."

Ultimately the train manoevered through some low hills and into sight of low-roofed houses across stretches of sand. Presently it stopped at a long wooden station. A score of Mexican urchins were congregated to see the arrival. Some twenty yards away stood a train composed of an engine, a mail and baggage car, a Pullman and three day coaches marked first, second and third class in Spanish. "There she is my boy," said the capitalist. "There's the Aztec limited. There's the train that's going to take us to the land of flowers and visions and all that."

There was a general charge upon the ticket office to get American money changed to Mexican money. It was a beautiful game. Two Mexican dollars were given for every American dollar. The passengers bid good-bye to their portraits of the national bird with exultant smiles. They examined with interest the new bills which were quite gay with red and purple and green. As for the silver dollar, the face of it intended to represent a cap of liberty with rays of glory shooting from it, but it looked to be on the contrary a picture of an exploding bomb. The capitalist from Chicago jingled his coin with glee. "Doubled my money.!"

"All aboard," said the conductor for the last time. Thereafter he said: "Vamanos." The train swung around the curve and toward the river. A soldier in blue fatigue uniform from the adjacent barracks, a portly German regardant at the entrance to his saloon, an elaborate and beautiful Anglo-Saxon oath from the top of a lumber pile, a vision of red and white and blue at the top of a distant staff, and the train was upon the high bridge that connects one nation with another.

Loredo appeared like a city veritably built upon sand. Little plats of vivid green grass appeared incredible upon this apparent waste. They looked like the grass mats of the theatrical stage. An old stone belfry arose above the low roofs. The river, shallow and quite narrow, flowed between wide banks of sand which seemed to express the stream's former records.

In Nuevo Laredo, there was a throng upon the platform—Mexican women, muffled in old shawls, and men, wrapped closely in dark-hued serapes. Over the heads of the men towered the peaked sombreros of fame. It was a preliminary picture painted in dark colors.

There was also a man in tan shoes and trousers of violent English check. When a gentleman of Spanish descent is important, he springs his knee-joint forward to its limit with each step. This gentleman was springing his knee-joints as if they were of no consequence, as if he had a new pair at his service.

"You have only hand baggage," said the conductor. "You won't have to get out."

Presently, the gentleman in tan shoes entered the car, springing his knee-joints frightfully. He caused the porter to let down all the upper berths while he fumbled among the blankets and matresses. The archaeologist and the capitalist had their valises already open and the gentleman paused in his knee-springing flight and gently peered in them. "All right," he said approvingly and pasted upon each of them a label which bore some formidable Mexican legend. Then he knee-springed himself away.

The train again invaded a wilderness of mesquite. It was amazing. The travellers had somehow expected a radical change the moment they were well across the Rio Grande. On the contrary, southern Texas was being repeated. They leaned close to the pane and stared into the mystic south. In the rear, however, Texas was represented by a long narrow line of blue hills, built up from the plain like a step.

Infrequently horsemen, shepherds, hovels appeared in the mesquite. Once, upon a small hillock a graveyard came into view and over each grave was a black cross. These somber emblems, lined against the pale sky, were given an inexpressibly mournful and fantastic horror from their color, new in this lonely land of brown bushes. The track swung to the westward and extended as straight as a rapier blade toward the rose-colored sky from whence the sun had vanished. The shadows of the mesquite deepened.

Presently the train passed at a village. Enough light remained to bring clearly into view some square yellow huts from whose rectangular doors there poured masses of crimson rays from the household fires. In these shimmering glows, dark and sinister shadows moved. The archaeologist and the capitalist were quite alone at this time in the sleeping-car and there was room for their enthusiasm, their ejaculations. Once they saw a black outline of a man upon one of these red canvasses. His legs were crossed, his arms were folded in his serape, his hat resembled a charlotte russe. He leaned negligently against the door-post. This figure justified to them all their preconceptions. He was more than a painting. He was the proving of certain romances, songs, narratives. He renewed their faith. They scrutinized him until the train moved away.

They wanted mountains. They clamored for mountains. "How soon, conductor, will we see any mountains?" The conductor indicated a long shadow in the pallor of the afterglow. Faint, delicate, it resembled the light rain-clouds of a faraway shower.

The train, rattling rhythmically, continued toward the far horizon. The deep mystery of night upon the mesquite prairie settled upon it like a warning to halt. The windows presented black expanses. At the little stations, calling voices could be heard from the profound gloom. Cloaked figures moved in the glimmer of lanterns.

The two travellers, hungry for color, form, action, strove to penetrate with their glances these black curtains of darkness which intervened between them and the new and strange life. At last, however, the capitalist settled down in the smoking compartment and recounted at length the extraordinary attributes of his children in Chicago.

Before they retired they went out to the platform and gazed into the south where the mountain range, still outlined against the soft sky, had grown portentously large. To those upon the trains, the black prairie seemed to heave like a sea and these mountains rose out of it like islands. In the west, a great star shone forth. "It is as large as a cheese," said the capitalist.

The archaeologist asserted the next morning that he had awakened at midnight and contemplated Monterey. It appeared, he said, as a high wall and a distant row of lights. When the capitalist awoke, the train was proceeding through a great wide valley which was radiant in the morning sunshine. Mountain ranges, wrinkled, crumpled, bare of everything save sage-brush, loomed on either side. Their little peaks were yellow in the light and their sides were of the faintest carmine tint, heavily interspersed with shadows. The wide, flat plain itself was grown thickly with sage-brush, but date palms were sufficiently numerous to make it look at times like a bed of some monstrous asparagus.

At every station a gorgeous little crowd had gathered to receive the train. Some were merely curious and others had various designs on the traveller—to beg from him or to sell to him. Indian women walked along the line of cars and held baskets of fruit toward the windows. Their broad, stolid faces were suddenly lit with a new commercial glow at the arrival of this trainful of victims. The men remained motionless and reposeful in their serapes. Back from the stations one could see the groups of white, flat-roofed adobe houses. From where a white road stretched over the desert toward the mountains, there usually arose a high, abiding cloud of dust from the hoofs of some cabellero's charger.

As this train conquered more and more miles towards its sunny destination, a regular progression in color could be noted. At Nuevo Laredo the prevailing tones in the dress of the people were brown, black and grey. Later an occasional purple or crimson serape was interpolated. And later still, the purple, the crimson and the other vivid hues became the typical colors, and even the trousers of dark cloth were replaced by dusty white cotton ones. A horseman in a red serape and a tall sombrero of maroon or pearl or yellow was vivid as an individual, but a dozen or two of them reposeful in the shade of some desert railway station made a chromatic delirium. In Mexico the atmosphere seldom softens anything. It devotes its energy to making high-lights, bringing everything forward, making colors fairly volcanic.

The bare feet of the women pattered to and fro along the row of car windows. Their cajoling voices were always soft and musical. The fierce sun of the desert beat down upon their baskets, wherein the fruit and food were exposed to each feverish ray.

From time to time across this lonely sunbeaten expanse, from which a storm of fine, dry dust ascended upon any provocation at all, the train passed walls made of comparatively small stones which extended for miles over the plain and then ascended the distant mountains in an undeviating line. They expressed the most incredible and apparently stupid labor. To see a stone wall beginning high and wide and extending to the horizon in a thin, monotonous thread, makes one think of the innumerable hands that toiled at the stones to divide one extent of sage-brush from another. Occasionally the low roof of a hacienda could be seen, surrounded by out-buildings and buried in trees. These walls marked the boundary of each hacienda's domain.

"Certain times of year," said the conductor, "there is nothing for the Indian peons to do, and as the rancheros have to feed 'em and keep 'em anyhow, you know, why they set 'em to building these stone walls."

The archaeologist and the capitalist gazed with a new interest at the groups of dusty-footed peons at the little stations. The clusters of adobe huts wherein some of them dwelt resembled the pictures of Palestine tombs. Withal, they smiled amiably, contentedly, their white teeth gleaming.

When the train roared past the stone monument that marked the Tropic of Cancer, the two travellers leaned out dangerously.

"Look at that, would you?"

"Well, I'm hanged!"

They stared at it with awed glances. "Well, well, so that's it, is it?" When the southern face of the monument was presented, they saw the legend, "Zona Torrida."

"Thunder, ain't this great."

Finally, the valley grew narrower. The track wound near the bases of hills. Through occasional passes could be seen other ranges, leaden-hued, in the distance. The sage-bushes became scarce and the cactus began to grow with a greater courage. The young green of other and unknown plants became visible. Greyish dust in swirl-ing masses marked the passage of the train.

At San Luis Potosi, the two travellers disembarked and again assailed one of those American restaurants which are located at convenient points. Roast chicken, tender steaks, chops, eggs, bis-cuit, pickles, cheese, pie, coffee, and just outside in blaring sunshine there was dust and Mexicans and a heathen chatter—a sort of an atmosphere of chili con carne, tortillas, tamales. The two travellers approached this table with a religious air as if they had encountered a shrine.

All the afternoon the cactus continued to improve in sizes. It now appeared that the natives made a sort of a picket fence of one va-

riety and shade trees from another. The brown faces of Indian
women and babes peered from these masses of prickly green.

At Atotonilco, a church with red-tiled towers appeared surrounded by poplar trees that resembled hearse plumes, and in the
stream that flowed near there was a multitude of heads with long
black hair. A vast variety of feminine garments decorated the
bushes that skirted the creek. A baby, brown as a water-jar and of
the shape of an alderman, paraded the bank in utter indifference or
ignorance or defiance.

At various times old beggars, grey and bent, tottered painfully
with out-stretched hats begging for centavos in voices that
expressed the last degree of chill despair. Their clothing hung in the
most supernatural tatters. It seemed miraculous that such fragments
could stay upon human bodies. With some unerring inexplainable
instinct they steered for the capitalist. He swore and blushed each
time. "They take me for an easy thing," he said wrathfully.
"No—I won't—get out—go away." The unmolested archaeologist
laughed.

The churches north of Monterey had been for the most part small
and meek structures surmounted by thin wooden crosses. They
were now more impressive, with double towers of stone and in the
midst of gardens and dependent buildings. Once the archaeologist
espied a grey and solemn ruin of a chapel. The old walls and belfry
appeared in the midst of a thicket of regardless cactus. He at once
recited to the capitalist the entire history of Cortez and the Aztecs.

At night-fall, the train paused at a station where the entire village
had come down to see it and gossip. There appeared to be no great
lighting of streets. Two or three little lamps burned at the station
and a soldier, or a policeman, carried a lantern which feebly illuminated his club and the bright steel of his revolver. In the profound
gloom, the girls walked arm and arm, three or four abreast, and
giggled. Bands of hoodlums scouted the darkness. One could hear
their shrill cat-calls. Some pedlers came with flaring torches and
tried to sell things.

In the early morning hours, the two travellers scrambled from
their berths to discover that the train was high in air. It had begun

its great climb of the mountains. Below and on the left, a vast plain of green and yellow fields was spread out like a checkered cloth. Here and there were tiny white villages, churches, haciendas. And beyond this plain arose the peak of Nevado de Toluca for 15,000 feet. Its eastern face was sun-smitten with gold and its snowy sides were shadowed with rose. The color of gold made it appear that this peak was staring with a high serene eternal glance into the East at the approach of the endless suns. And no one feels like talking in the presence of these mountains that stand like gods on the world, for fear that they might hear. Slowly the train wound around the face of the cliff.

When you come to this country, do not confuse the Mexican cakes with pieces of iron ore. They are not pieces of iron ore. They are cakes.

At a mountain station to which the train had climbed in some wonderful fashion, the travellers breakfasted upon cakes and coffee. The conductor, tall, strong, as clear-headed and as clear-eyed, as thoroughly a type of the American railroad man, as if he were in charge of the Pennsylvania Limited, sat at the head of the table and harangued the attendant peon. The capitalist took a bite of cake and said "Gawd!"

This little plateau was covered with yellow grass which extended to the bases of the hills that were on all sides. These hills were grown thickly with pines, fragrant, gently waving in the cool breeze. Upon the station platform a cavalry officer, under a grey sombrero heavily ladened with silver braid, conversed with a swarthy trooper. Over the little plain, a native in a red blanket was driving a number of small donkeys who were each carrying an enormous load of fresh hay.

The conductor again yelled out a password to a Chinese lodge and the train renewed its attack upon these extraordinary ridges which intervened between it and its victory. The passengers prepared themselves. Every car window was hung full of heads that were for the most part surmounted by huge sombreros. A man, with such a large roll of matting strapped to his back that he looked like a perambulating sentry-box, leaned upon his staff in the roadway and stared at the two engines. Puffing, panting, heaving, they strained like thoroughbred animals with every steel muscle of their bodies and slowly the train was hauled up this tilted track.

In and out among the hills it went, higher and higher. Often two steel rails were visible far below on the other side of a ravine. It seemed incredible that ten minutes before the train had been at that place.

In the depths of the valley, a brook brawled over the rocks. A man in dusty white garments lay asleep in the shade of a pine.

At last the whistle gave a triumphant howl. The summit—10,000 feet above the sea—was reached. A winding slide, a sort of tremendous toboggan affair, began. Around and around among the hills glided the train. Little flat white villages displayed themselves in the valleys. The maguey plant, from which the Mexicans make their celebrated tanglefoot, flourished its lance-point leaves in long rows. The hills were checkered to their summits with brown fields. The train swinging steadily down the mountains crossed one stream thirteen times on bridges dizzily high.

Suddenly two white peaks, afar off, raised above the horizon, peering over the ridge. The capitalist nearly fell off the train. Popocatepetl and Ixtaccihuatl, the two giant mountains, clothed in snow that was like wool, were marked upon the sky. A glimpse was had of a vast green plain. In this distance, the castle of Chapultepec resembled a low thunder cloud.

Presently the train was among long white walls, green lawns, high shade trees. The passengers began their preparations for disembarking as the train manoevered through the switches. At last there came a depot heavily fringed with people, an omnibus, a dozen cabs and a soldier in a uniform that fitted him like a bird cage. White dust arose high toward the blue sky. In some tall grass on the other side of the track, a little cricket suddenly chirped. The two travellers with shining eyes climbed out of the car. "A-a-ah," they said in a prolonged sigh of delight. The city of the Aztecs was in their power.

8. Stephen Crane in Mexico: II

City of Mexico, May 18.—

Two Americans were standing on a street corner in this city not long ago, gazing thoughtfully at the paintings on the exterior wall of a pulque shop—stout maidens in scant vestments lovingly confronting a brimming glass, kings out of all proportion draining goblets to more stout maidens—the whole a wild mass of red, green, blue, yellow, purple, like a concert hall curtain in a mining town.

Far up the street six men in white cotton shirts and short trousers became visible. They were bent forward and upon their shoulders there was some kind of an enormous black thing. They moved at a shambling trot.

The two Americans lazily wondered about the enormous black thing, but the distance defeated them. The six men, however, were approaching at an unvarying pace, and at last one American was enabled to cry out: "Holy poker, it's a piano!"

There was a shuffling sound of sandals upon the stones. In the vivid yellow sun-light the black surface of the piano glistened. The six brown faces were stolid and unworried beneath it.

They passed. The burden and its carriers grew smaller and smaller. The two Americans went out to the curb and remained intent spectators until the six men and the piano were expressed by a faint blur.

When you first come to Mexico and you see a donkey so loaded that little of him but a furry nose and four short legs appear to the eye, you wonder at it. Later, when you see a hay-stack approaching

STEPHEN CRANE IN MEXICO | [rule] | Author of "The Black Riders" on Street | Porters and Venders. | [rule] | THE PATIENT, PATHETIC BURRO | [rule] | A City Where Many Things Are Pass- | ing Strange, but Where You | Can, After All, Get a Man- | hattan Cocktail. | [rule] | (Copyright, 1895.)

with nothing under it but a pair of thin human legs, you begin to understand the local point of view. The Indian probably reasons: "Well, I can carry this load. The burro, then, he should carry many times this much." The burro, born in slavery, dying in slavery, generation upon generation, he with his wobbly legs, sore back, and ridiculous little face, reasons not at all. He carries as much as he can, and when he can carry it no further, he falls down.

The Indians, however, must have credit for considerable ingenuity because of the way they have invented of assisting a fallen donkey to its feet. The Aztecs are known to have had many great mechanical contrivances, and this no doubt is part of their science which has filtered down through the centuries.

When a burdened donkey falls down a half dozen Indians gather around it and brace themselves. Then they take clubs and hammer the everlasting day-lights out of the donkey. They also swear in Mexican. Mexican is a very capable language for the purposes of profanity. A good swearer here can bring rain in thirty minutes.

It is a great thing to hear the thump, thump, of the clubs and the howling of the natives, and to see the little legs of the donkey quiver and to see him roll his eyes. Finally, after they have hammered him out as flat as a drum head, it flashes upon them suddenly that the burro cannot get up and they remove his load. Well, then, at last, they remove his load and the donkey, not much larger than a kitten at best, and now disheveled, weak and tottering, struggles gratefully to his feet.

But, on the other hand, it is possible to see at times—perhaps in the shade of an old wall where branches hang over and look down—the tender communion of two sympathetic spirits. The man pats affectionately the soft muzzle of the donkey. The donkey—ah, who can describe that air so sage, so profoundly reflective, and yet so kind, so forgiving, so unassuming. The countenance of a donkey expresses all manly virtues even as the sunlight expresses all colors.

Perhaps the master falls asleep, and, in that case, the donkey still stands as immovable, as patient, as the stone dogs that guarded the temple of the sun.

A wonderful proportion of the freight-carrying business of this city is conducted by the Indian porters. The donkeys are the great general freight cars and hay wagons for the rural districts, but they do not appear prominently in the strictly local business of the city. It is a strange fact also that of ten wagons that pass you upon the street nine will be cabs and private carriages. The tenth may be a huge American wagon belonging to one of the express companies. It is only fair to state, however, that the odds are in favor of it being another cab or carriage.

The transportation of the city's goods is then left practically in the hands of the Indian porters. They are to be seen at all times trotting to and fro, laden and free. They have acquired all manner of contrivances for distributing the weight of their burdens. Their favorite plan is to pass a broad band over their foreheads and then, leaning forward precariously, they amble along with the most enormous loads.

Sometimes they have a sort of table with two handles on each end. Two men, of course, manage this machine. It is the favorite vehicle for moving furniture.

When a man sits down who has been traversing a long road with a heavy bundle he would find considerable agony in the struggle to get upon his feet again with his freight strapped to his back if it were not for a long staff which he carries. He plants the point of this staff on the ground between his knees, and then climbs up it, so to speak, hand over hand.

They have undoubtedly developed what must be called the carrying instinct. Occasionally you may see a porter, unburdened, walking unsteadily as if his center of balance had been shuffled around so much that he is doubtful. He resembles then an unballasted ship. Place a trunk upon his back and he is as steady as a church.

If you put in his care a contrivance with fifty wheels he would not trundle it along the ground. This plan would not occur to him. No, he would shoulder it. Most bicycles are light enough in weight, but they are rather unhandy articles to carry for long distances. Yet if you send one by a porter he will most certainly carry it on his shoulder. It would fatigue him to roll it along the road.

But there are other things odd here beside the street porters. Yesterday some thieves stole three iron balconies from off the second-story front of a house in the Calle de Sol. The police did not catch the miscreants. Who, indeed, is instructed in the art of catching thieves who steal iron balconies from the second-story fronts of houses?

The people directly concerned went out in the street and assured themselves that the house remained. Then they were satisfied.

As a matter of truth, the thieves of the city are almost always petty fellows, who go about stealing trifling articles and spend much time and finesse in acquiring things that a dignified American crook wouldn't kick with his foot. In truth, the City of Mexico is really one of the safest cities in the world at any hour of the day or night. However, the small-minded and really harmless class who vend birds, canes, opals, lottery tickets, paper flowers and general merchandise upon the streets are able and industrious enough in the art of piracy to satisfy the ordinary intellect.

Those profound minds who make the guide books have warned the traveller very lucidly. After exhaustive thought, the writer has been able to deduct the following elementary rules from what they have to say upon the matter:

I. Do not buy anything at all from street venders.

II. When buying from street venders give the exact sum charged. Do not delude yourself with the idea of getting any change back.

III. When buying from street venders divide by ten the price demanded for any article, and offer it.

IV. Do not buy anything at all from street venders.

It is not easy to go wrong when you have one of these protective volumes within reach, but then the guide book has long been subject to popular ridicule and there is not the universal devotion to its pages which it clearly deserves. Strangers upon entering Mexico should at once acquire a guide book, and then, if they fail to gain the deepest knowledge of the country and its inhabitants, they may lay it to their own inability to understand the English language in its purest form. There are tourists now in this hotel who have only been in the city two days, but who, in this time, have devoted themselves so earnestly to their guide books that they are able to draw maps of how Mexico looked before the flood.

It is never just to condemn a class and, in returning to the street venders, it is but fair to record an extraordinary instance of the gentleness, humanity and fine capability of pity in one of their number. An American lady was strolling in a public park one afternoon when she observed a vender with four little plum-colored birds seated quietly and peacefully upon his brown hand.

"Oh look at those dear little birds," she cried to her escort. "How tame they are!"

Her escort, too, was struck with admiration and astonishment and they went close to the little birds. They saw their happy, restful countenances and with what wealth of love they looked up into the face of their owner.

The lady bought two of these birds, although she hated to wound their little hearts by tearing them away from their master.

When she got to her room she closed the door and the windows, and then reached into the wicker cage and brought out one of the pets, for she wished to gain their affection, too, and teach them to sit upon her finger.

The little bird which she brought out made a desperate attempt to perch upon her finger, but suddenly toppled off and fell to the floor with a sound like that made by a water-soaked bean bag.

The loving vender had filled his birds full of shot. This accounted for their happy, restful countenances and their very apparent resolution never to desert the adored finger of their master.

In an hour both the little birds died. You would die too if your stomach was full of shot.

The men who sell opals are particularly seductive. They polish their wares and boil them in oil, and do everything to give them a false quality. When they come around in the evening and unfold a square of black paper, revealing a little group of stones that gleam with green and red fires, it is very dispiriting to know that if one bought one would be cheated.

The other day a vender unholding a scarfpin of marvelous brilliancy approached a tourist.

"How much?" demanded the latter.

"Twelve dollars," replied the vender. "Cheap! Very Cheap! Only $12."

The tourist looked at the stone and then said: "Twelve dollars! No! One dollar."

"Yes, yes," cried the vender eagerly. "One dollar! Yes, yes; you can have it for $1. Take it!"

But the tourist laughed and passed on.

The fact remains, however, that the hotels, the restaurants and the cabs are absolutely cheap and almost always fair. If a man consults reputable shopkeepers when he wishes to buy Mexican goods, and gives a proper number of hours each day to the study of guide books, the City of Mexico is a place of joy. The climate is seldom hot and seldom cold. And to those gentlemen from the States whose minds have a sort of liquid quality, it is necessary merely to say that if you go out into the street and yell: "Gimme a Manhattan!" about forty American bartenders will appear of a sudden and say: "Yes, sir."

9. In Free Silver Mexico

City of Mexico, June 29.—
Mexico is a free silver country. When travellers from the United States arrive at Laredo, or at Eagle Pass, or at El Paso, they, of

---

IN FREE SILVER MEXICO | [rule] | How the White Metal Standard Affects |Wages and Living. | [rule]| AN IMPORTANT MATTER DISCUSSED |[rule]| Stephen Crane Finds that Twice as | Many Jingling Dollars Won't | Begin to Buy Twice as | Many Things. | [rule] | (Copyright, 1895, by Bacheller, Johnson & Bacheller.)

course, exchange their American coin for the currency of Mexico. In place of the green bills of the United States they receive the rather gaudy script of Mexico. For the silver of the American eagle they receive dollars which bear imprints of the eagle, serpent and cactus of this brown republic of the south. It makes them feel very wealthy. The rate of exchange is always about two for one. For fifty American dollars they receive one hundred of the dollars of Mexico. It is a great thing to double money in this fashion. The American tourist is likely to keep his hand in his pocket and jingle his horde.

However, when he boards the Pullman to ride to the City of Mexico he finds that the fare has become nine dollars in Mexican money, instead of the normal and expected $4.50. The traveller discovers that he has not as yet gained anything. Still greater is his disappointment when he learns that the usual tip to the porter is now fifty cents, instead of the almost universal quarter. He exclaims that he can as yet see no benefit in this money exchange.

The Americans who earn salaries in the City of Mexico are continually crying that if they could only get their pay in American money and spend it in Mexican money they would be happy. A Mexican dollar is a good dollar with which to buy things, unless those things be imported. Then there is trouble. Pullman cars, porters and a multitude of other things which will be enumerated hereafter come very high.

If a young Mexican clerk, who is, for instance, on a salary of $60 per month, but who, nevertheless, thinks considerable of himself, as young clerks are apt to do—if this young clerk wishes to purchase a suit of clothes commensurate with his opinions, he will have to spend something more than a month's pay to get it. If he wishes to buy a good pair of trousers, he is required to pay about $15. Hats are to be bought at about $10. A tie—an ordinary four-in-hand—comes at $1. A collar is a matter of 35 cents. The best brand costs 50 cents. A pair of cuffs can be obtained in exchange for 60 cents. Shoes, which are ordinarily of very poor quality, cost from $8 to $20. Young clerks do not become great dudes in Mexico.

It is to be noticed that the best-dressed men in Mexico are not nearly so well dressed as the men of an ordinary New York crowd.

Of course, one would expect the styles to be old, but then there is to be observed a certain lack of quality to the cloths, an air of being fragile about the shoes, and as for the hats, anything goes in Mexico.

The lower classes in Mexico do not wear shoes. They seem contented enough in their sandals, but if one of them should save his money in order to buy a pair of shoes, it would take about ten years for him to get the required amount. That is to say, if he got paid at the usual Mexican rates.

If a man wishes to see his wife and his daughters well dressed and in the latest Mexican style, it costs him a very pretty penny. It is not in the power of the middle-class Mexican to buy gowns for the feminine part of his family, as a middle-class American may do. He would go broke shortly.

It costs 25 cents to get shaved in a Mexican city. However, there is one great point where the Mexicans head us. Cocktails are sold at the rate of two for a Mexican quarter. All the good brands of whisky are at the same rate. Reduced to an American standard, this is at the rate of 6 1/4 cents per cocktail or per whisky. Beer is sold for 10 cents a glass—in American terms 5 cents a glass. The beer is not imported, but the whiskies come straight from the United States and Canada. Still, whisky is cheaper in Oaxaca or Tehuantepec than it is in Kentucky. There are quite a number of Kentucky emigrants to Mexico who do not feel that longing to return to the homes of their fathers which one would naturally expect in a true-born son of the blue-grass State.

Railroad fares in Mexico are usually quoted at double the mileage in the United States. That is to say, reduced to a common basis, they are equivalent. This doubling of the rates, then, does not affect the tourist from the United States, because he thinks in American coin, but it plays havoc with the Mexican citizen, who earns his money in the coin of Mexico. The passenger trains of these railroads carry first, second and third class coaches. One can find very well-mannered and sensitive people in the second-class car. As for the Pullman, it is the resort of the Americans, and of the higher, perhaps only the very swellest and most wealthy, grade of Mexicans.

Perhaps it should have been mentioned some distance back in this article that the lower classes can purchase pulque, the native beverage, at the rate of 3 cents per glass. Five glasses seem to be sufficient to floor the average citizen of the republic, so it happens that he can get howling, staggering and abusive for 15 cents, or, in our money, 7 1/2 cents.

The author of this article is not to be supposed to be transfixed with admiration because of the above facility of jag. He merely recites facts. It is a national condition, for which he is in no wise responsible.

The cost of prepared foods in Mexico is, when reduced to a common basis, about the same as it is in the United States. If one goes to an American restaurant in Mexico, he gets robbed more or less, but then this is not important. The Mexicans themselves live cheaply. However, they do not have one-eighth of the comforts and luxury that are in the ordinary little American home. Their lives in their houses are bare and scant, when measured with American firesides.

The Mexican laborer earns from 1 real (6 1/4 cents United States) to 4 reals (25 cents United States) per day. He lives mostly on frijoles, which are beans. His clothing consists of a cotton shirt, cotton trousers, leather sandals, and a straw hat. For his wages he has to work like a horse.

10. A Jag of Pulque is Heavy

City of Mexico, Aug. 4, 1895.—
The first thing to be done by the investigating tourist of this country

---

A JAG OF PULQUE IS HEAVY. | [rule] |A Country Where a Drink Will Fill One's | Vision With Sea Serpents. | [rule]| Stephen Crane Describes the Hor- | rors of Pulque and Registers a | Few Eloquent Vows—Inebriety | in the City of Mexico. | [rule]

is to begin to drink the national beverage, pulque. The second thing to be done by the investigating tourist is to cease to drink pulque. This last recommendation, however, is necessary to no one. The human inclination acts automatically, so to speak, in this case. If the great drunkard of the drama should raise his right hand and swear solemnly never to touch another drop of intoxicating pulque as long as he lived—so help him heaven—he would make himself ridiculous. It would be too simple. Why should a man ever taste another drop of pulque after having once collided with it?

But this does not relate to the Mexicans. This relates to the foreigner who brings with him numerous superstitions and racial, fundamental traditions concerning odors. To the foreigner, the very proximity of a glass of pulque is enough to take him up by the hair and throw him violently to the ground.

It resembles green milk. The average man has never seen green milk, but if he can imagine a handful of paris green interpolated into a glass of cream, he will have a fair idea of the appearence of pulque. And it tastes like—it tastes like—some terrible concoction of bad yeast perhaps. Or maybe some calamity of eggs.

This, bear in mind, represents the opinion of a stranger. As far as the antagonism of the human stomach goes, there can be no doubt but that pulque bears about the same relation to the uninitiated sense as does American or any kind of beer. But the first encounter is a revelation. One understands then that education is everything, even as the philosophers say, and that we would all be eating sandwiches made from door-mats if only circumstances had been different.

To the Mexican, pulque is a delirium of joy. The lower classes dream of pulque. There are pulque shops on every corner in some quarters of the city. And, lined up at the bar in conventional fashion, the natives may be seen at all times, yelling thirsty sentences at the barkeepers. These pulque shops are usually decorated both inside and out with the real old paintings done on the walls by the hand of some unknown criminal. Looking along the pale walls of the streets, one is startled at every corner by these sudden lurid interjections of pulque green, red, blue, yellow. The pulque is served in little brown earthen mugs that are shaped in miniature precisely like one of the famous jars of the orient.

The native can get howling full for anything from twelve cents to twenty cents. Twelve cents is the equivalent in American coinage of about six cents. Many men of celebrated thirsts in New York would consider this a profoundly ideal condition. However, six cents represents something to the Indian. Unless there are some Americans around to be robbed, he is obliged to rustle very savagely for his pulque money. When he gets it he is happy and the straight line he makes for one of the flaming shops has never been outdone by any metropolitan iceman that drinks. In the meantime the swarm of pulque saloons are heavily taxed, and the aggregate amount of their payments to the government is almost incredible. The Indian, in his dusty cotton shirt and trousers, his tattered sombrero, his flapping sandals, his stolid dark face, is of the same type in this regard that is familiar to every land, the same prisoner, the same victim.

In riding through almost any part of this high country, you will pass acre after acre, mile after mile, of "century" plants laid out in rows that stretch always to the horizon whether it is at the hazy edge of a mighty plain or at the summit of a rugged and steep mountain. You wonder at the immensity of the thing. Haciendas will have their thousands of acres planted in nothing but the maguey, or, as the Americans call it, the "century" plant. The earth is laid out in one tremendous pattern, maguey plants in long sweeping perspective.

Well, it is from this plant that the natives make pulque.

Pulque is the juice taken from the heart of the maguey and allowed to ferment for one day. After that time, it must be consumed within twenty-four hours or it is positively useless. The railroads that run through the principal maguey districts operate fast early-morning pulque trains in much the same fashion that the roads that run through Orange Co., N.Y., operate early-morning milk trains to New York. From the depots it is hustled in wagons and on the backs of porters to the innumerable saloons and from thence dispensed to the public.

Mescal and tequila are two native rivals of pulque. Mescal is a sort of a cousin of whisky, although to the eye it is as clear as water, and tequila is to mescal as brandy is to whisky. They are both wrung from the heart of the maguey plant. In a low part of the country where pulque cannot be produced the natives use mescal, for this beverage is of course capable of long journeys, but where a native can get pulque he usually prefers it.

The effects of pulque as witnessed in the natives does not seem to be so pyrotechnic and clamorous as are the effects of certain other drinks upon the citizens of certain other nations. The native, filled with pulque, seldom wishes to fight. Usually he prefers to adore his friends. They will hang together in front of a bar, three or four of them, their legs bending, their arms about each other's necks, their faces lit with an expression of the most ideal affection and supreme brotherly regard. It would be difficult to make an impression on their feelings at those times with a club. Their whole souls are completely absorbed in this beatific fraternal tenderness.

Still, there are certain mixtures, certain combinations, which invariably breed troubles. Let the native mix his pulque at three cents a glass with some of that vivid native brandy and there is likely to be a monstrous turmoil on little or no provocation. Out at Santa Anita, which is a resort for the upper classes on the Viga canal, they used to have a weekly ceremony which was of the same order as the regular Sunday night murder in the old days of Mulberry Bend. And it happened because the natives mixed their drinks.

11. The Dress of Old Mexico

The hat is the main strength of the true Mexican dude. Upon these gorgeous sombreros the Mexican gentleman of fashion frequently

THE DRESS OF OLD MEXICO |[rule]|Stephen Crane Writes of Amazing Hats, | Shirts and Spurs. | [rule] | THE MEXICAN'S LARGE CHAPEAU | [rule] | Americans and English Ideas Slowly | Reaching the people of the Towns|—Color Still Supreme in|the Country.|[rule] [At the foot of this article is Copyright, 1896.]

spends $50 or even a hundred dollars. And these splendid masses of gold braid and pearl grey beaver surmount the average masculine head with the same artistic value as would a small tower of bricks. In the first place, the true Mexican wears his trousers very tight in the leg, and as his legs are always small and wiry, he produces an effect of instability. When you see him crowned by one of those great peaked sombreros, you think he is likely to fall down upon slight occasion.

This same gentleman may run to spurs a good deal. There are for sale in the shops in the City of Mexico silver spurs that weigh a couple of pounds each—immense things that look more like rhinocerous traps than spurs to urge on a horse. He may, too, when he rides in the country, have a pair of elegantly decorated pistol holsters at his pommel. A double row of little silver buttons extend down each leg of his tight trousers and it is more than probable that his little jacket will be embroidered like mad. After all this, he will be seated upon a saddle that the sultan of a thousand Turkeys would never dare use for a foot-stool. Mounted then upon a charger that proceeds at mincing, restrained gait down the avenue crowded with fashionable carriages, he, with his full chin, black moustache, and vaguely sinister eye, is the true type of the Mexican caballeo.

But, on the other hand, the true Mexican style has been combated subtly for years by the ideas from America and from Europe, which have flown into the country. In the rural districts the caballero is still supreme, but in the larger towns and in the capital the men of the greatest wealth and position always resemble the ordinary type of American men of affairs. And the younger generation, who are yet of a mind to care for dress, study the fashions of New York and London with much diligence.

Here begins the conflict between the holy London creed of what is correct and an inate love of vivid personal adornment. They clash and the clash is sometimes to be heard for miles. The great distance which these mandates come also confuses matters.

Here is an attempt at a typical enumeration:

I. A black tie, a high white collar, a green opal stud in a shirt of crimson silk.

II. Cuffs of fine lace, a shirt bosom of more fine lace which falls in a beautiful cascade over the breast of a descreet black cutaway.

III. Four men in evening dress at 10:30 a.m.

IV. A shirt with green stripes two inches wide and red four-in-hand tie.

V. A tie of blue China silk, the ends of which fall to the waist.

These effects are to be seen from time to time. It would not be reasonable to quarrel with them or sneer at them. The first young man has an absolute right to wear his crimson shirt if it does not burn him. He no doubt finds it decorative and comfortable. Perhaps his sisters think it admirable and perhaps some señorita with flashing eyes thinks nothing so handsome as that little triangle of crimson, which glows above his coat lapels. It is never wise to deride the fashions of another people for we ourselves have no idea of what we are coming to. Within two years, New York may be absolutely on fire with crimson shirts—blood red bosoms may flash in the air like lanterns.

Occasionally, in strolls about the streets one is able to observe the final development of the English check. When a man sincerely sets out to have a suit of checked cloth, it is astonishing to what an extent he can carry his passion. There are suits of this description here that in the vivid sun-light of the country throw a checkered shadow upon the pavement. They are usually upon Mexicans of the lower middle-class, who save them for afternoon strolls. I distinctly remember some window shades to a store in upper Broadway that I thought displayed the most devastating checks in the universe.

They do not.

But above all the reader must remember that the great mass of humanity upon the principal business street of Mexico City dress about the same as they do in other places. There is a little more variety perhaps and of course there is an interpolation of Indians, who are utterly distinct. But in the main there is a great similarity. The streets do not blaze. If you wish to blaze go into side streets where the Indians live.

The Indian remains the one great artistic figure. But the Indian in his serape, with his cotton trousers, his dusty sandals upon which his bare toes are displayed, and his old sombrero pulled down over his eyes, is a fascinating man.

Whether this blanket is purple or not or of some dull hue, he fits into green grass, the low white walls, the blue sky, as if his object was not so much to get possession of some centavos as to compose the picture.

At night, when he crouches in a doorway with his sombrero pulled still further over his eyes, and his mouth covered by a fold of his serape, you can imagine anything at all about him for his true character is impenetrable. He is a mystic and silent figure of the darkness.

He has two great creeds. One is that pulque as a beverage is finer than the melted blue of the sky. The other is that Americans are eternally wealthy and immortally stupid. If the world was really of the size that he believes it to be, you could put his hat over it.

12. The Main Streets of this City

City of Mexico,

The main streets of this city do not preserve the uniform uproar that marks the daily life of the important thoroughfares in northern cities. Their life begins at an early hour and lasts until almost noon. Then there is a period of repose. Few people appear upon the sidewalks and barely a carriage obstructs the assault of the glaring yellow sun-light upon the pave of the street. At about 3.30, however, there is an awakening. Carriages come from all directions. The walks are suddenly thick with people and from that time until 9.00 the streets are a-whirl with shining carriages, sombrero-ed coachmen, proud horses. A mighty gathering of young men crowd the curbs and peer at the occupants of the passing vehicles. The blue quivering light of the modern electric lamp illuminates the fine old decorations of the buildings and above all rings the clatter of innumerable hoofs upon the concrete of the narrow streets.

Or perhaps instead of the period of glaring sun-light there comes a swift and sudden rain with the premonitory winds, the atmospheric coolness, the low-hanging deep-blue clouds, the rumbling thunder of a spring shower in the north. Then as soon as the rain ceases, the carriages, like some kind of congregating bugs, come flying again. In the parks, the vivid green of the foliage turns dark from the shadows of the night.

The term "rainy season" in the City of Mexico merely means that a certain time every afternoon you can count upon a shower that will last for an hour or more. It is as regular almost as day and night and you have only to make your arrangements according to it. During the winter, the weather is immovably calm. Each day is the counterpart of the day that precedes it. You could make picnic plans weeks in advance and be sure of your weather. It is precisely like late spring as we of the north know it.

This gives the belles of the city no opportunity to exploit those enormous capes which make every woman look like a full-rigged ship going before the wind. They would be smothered. But still they can wear Easter bonnets all the time. In fact, one is always able to see upon the streets those fresh and charming toilettes which we associate with the new blossoming of womanhood in the spring.

The Mexican women are beautiful frequently but there seems to be that quality lacking which makes the bright quick eyes of some girls so adorable to the contemplative sex. It has something to do with the mind, no doubt. Their black eyes are as beautiful as gems. The trouble with the gem however is that it cannot regard you with sudden intelligence, comprehension, sympathy. They have soft rounded cheeks which they powder without much skill, leaving it often in streaks. They take life easily, dreamily. They remind one of kittens asleep in the sunshine.

The stranger to the city is at once interested in the architecture of the buildings. They are not ruins but they have somehow the dignity of ruins. There is probably no structure in the city of the character that a man of the north would erect. Viewing them as a mass, they are two-storied and plain with heavily barred windows from which the señorita can gaze down at the street. In the principal part of the town, however, there are innumerable fine old houses with large shaded courts and simple stern decorations that must be echoes of the talent of the Aztecs. There is nothing of the modern in them. They are never incoherent, never over-done. The ornamentation is always a part of the structure. It grows there. It has not been plastered on from a distance. Galleries wind about the sides of the silent and shadowed patios.

Commerce has however waged a long war upon these structures and a vast number of them have succumbed. Signs are plastered on their exteriors and the old courts are given over to the gentle hum of Mexican business. It is not unusual for the offices of a commission merchant or of a dealer of any kind to be located in a building that was once the palace of some Mexican notable and the massive doors, the broad stair-way, the wide galleries, have become in this strange evolution as familiar to messenger boys and porters as they were once perhaps to generals and statesmen. The old palace of the Emperor Iturbide is now a hotel over-run with American tourists. The Mexican National Railroad has its general offices in a building that was the palace of a bygone governor of the city and the American Club has the finest of club-houses because it gained control of a handsome old palace.

There is a certain American aspect to the main business part of the town. Men with undeniable New England faces confront one constantly. The business signs are often American and there is a little group of cafes where everything from the aprons of the waiters to the liquids dispensed are American. One hears in this neighborhood more English than Spanish. Even the native business purpose changes under this influence and they bid for the American coin. "American Barber-shop," "The American Tailor," "American Restaurant" are signs which flatter the tourist's eye. There is nothing so universal as the reputation of Americans for ability to spend money. There can be no doubt that the Zulus upon the approach of an American citizen begin to lay all manner of traps.

Nevertheless there is a sort of a final adjustment. There is an American who runs a merry-go-round in one of the parks here. It is the usual device with a catarrhal orchestrion and a whirl of wooden goats, and ponies and giraffes. But his machine is surrounded at all times by fascinated natives and he makes money by the basketful. The circus too, which is really a more creditable organization than any we see in the states, is crowded nightly. It is a small circus. It does not attempt to have simultaneous performances in fifty-nine rings but everything is first-class and the American circus people attain reputations among the populace second only to the most adored of the bull-fighters.

The bull-fighters, by the way, are a most impressive type to be seen upon the streets. There is a certain uniformity about their apparel. They wear flat-topped glazed hats like the seamen of years ago and little short jackets. They are always clean-shaven and the set of the lips, wherein lies the revelation of character, can easily be studied. They move confidently, proudly, with a magnificent self-possession. People turn to stare after them. There is in their faces something cold, sinister, merciless. There is history there too, a history of fiery action, of peril, of escape. Yet you would know, you would know without being told, that you are gazing at an executioner, a kind of moral assassin.

The faces of the priests are perhaps still more portentous, for the countenances of the bull-fighters are obvious but those of the priests are inscrutable.

13.   The Viga Canal

City of Mexico,
The Viga Canal leads out to the floating gardens. The canal is really
a canal but the floating gardens are not floating gardens at all. We
took a cab and rattled our bones loose over the stones of streets
where innumerable natives in serape and sombrero thronged about
pulque shops that were also innumerable. Brown porters in cotton
shirts and trousers trotted out of the way of the cab, moving huge
burdens with rare ease. The women, seated upon the curb with
their babes, glanced up at the rumble of wheels. There were
dashes of red and purple from the clothes of the people against the
white and yellow background of the low adobe buildings. Into the
clear cool afternoon air arose the squawling cries of the vendors
of melons, saints, flowers.

At the canal, there was a sudden fierce assault of boatmen that
was like a charge of desperate infantry. Behind them their boats
crowded each other at the wharf and the canal lay placid to where,
upon the further shore, long lazy blades of grass bended to the
water like swooning things. At the pulque shop, the cabman paused
for a drink before his return drive.

The boatmen beseeched, prayed, appealed. There could have
been no more clamor around the feet of the ancient brown gods of
Mexico. They almost shed tears; they wriggled in an ecstasy of
commercial expectation. They smote their bare breasts and each
swore himself to be the incomparable boatman of the Viga. Above
their howls arose the thinkle of a street-car bell as the driver lashed
his mules toward the city.

The fortunate boatman fairly trembled in his anxiety to get his
craft out into the canal before his freight could change their minds.
He pushed frantically with his pole and the boat, built precisely like
what we call a scow, moved slowly away.

Great trees lined the shore. The little soiled street-cars passed and passed. Far along the shimmering waters, on which details of the foilage were traced, could be seen countless boatmen, erect in the sterns of their crafts, bending and swaying rhythmically, prodding the bottom with long poles. Out from behind the corner of a garden-wall suddenly appeared Popocatapetl, towering toward the sky, a great cone of creamy hue in the glamor of the sunshine. Then later came Ixtaccihuatl, the white woman, of curious shape, more camel than woman, its peak confused with clouds. A plain of fervent green stretched toward them. On the other side of the canal, in the shade of a great tree, a mounted gendarme sat immovable and contemplative.

A little canoe, made from the trunk of a single tree and narrower than a coffin, approached and the Indian girl in the bow advocated the purchase of tamales while in the stern a tall youth in scant clothing poled away keeping pace with the larger craft.

Frequently there were races. Reposing under the wooden canopies of the boats, people cried to their boatmen. "Hurry up! If you beat that boat ahead, I will give you another real." The laconic Spanish sentences, fortified usually with swift gestures, could always be heard. And under the impetus of these offers the boatmen struggled hardily, their sandaled feet pattering as they ran along the sides of the boats.

There were often harmless collisions. These boatmen, apparently made blind by the prospective increase in reward, poled sometimes like mad and crashed into boats ahead. Then arose the fervor of Mexican oaths.

Withal, however, they were very skilful, managing their old wooden boxes better than anybody could ever expect of them. And indeed some of them were clever enough to affect the most heroic exertions and gain more pay when in reality they were not injuring their health at all.

At the little village of Santa Anita, everybody disembarked. There was a great babbling crowd in front of the pulque shops. Vivid serapes lighted the effect made by the modest and very economical cotton clothes of the most of the people. In the midst of this uproar, three more mounted gendarmes sat silently, their sabres dangling in their scabbards, their horses poising their ears intently at the throng.

Indian girls with bare brown arms held up flowers for sale, flowers of flaming colors made into wreaths and bouquets. Caballeros, out for a celebration, a carouse, strutted along with these passionate burning flowers of the southland serving as bands to their sombreros. Under the thatched roofs of the pulque shops, more Indian girls served customers with the peculiar beverage and stood by and bantered with them in the universal style. In the narrow street leading away from the canal, the crowd moved hilariously while crouched at the sides of it a multitude of beggars, decrepit vendors of all kinds, raised unheeded cries. In the midst of the swarming pulque shops, resorts, and gardens, stood a little white church, stern, unapproving, representing the other fundamental aspiration of humanity, a reproach and a warning. The frightened laughter of a girl in a swing could be heard as her lover swung her high, so that she appeared for a moment in her fluttering blue gown and tossing locks over a fence of tall cactus plants.

A policeman remonstrated with a tottering caballero who wished to kiss a waitress in a pulque shop. A boatman, wailing bitterly, shambled after some riotous youths who had forgotten to pay him. Four men seated around a table were roaring with laughter at the tale of a fifth man. Three old Indian women with bare shoulders and wondrously wrinked faces squatted on the earthen floor of a saloon and watched the crowd. Little beggars beseeched everybody. "Niña! Niña! Deme un centavo!"

Above the dark formidable hills of the west there was a long flare of crimson, purple, orange, tremendous colors that, in the changes of the sunset, manoevred in the sky like armies. Suddenly the little church aroused and its bell clanged persistently, harshly and with an incredible rapidity. People were beginning to saunter back toward the canal.

We procured two native musicians, a violinist and a guitarist, and took them with us in our boat. The shadows of the trees in the water grew more portentous. Far to the southeast the two peaks were faint ghostly figures in the heavens. They resembled forms of silver mist in the deep blue of that sky. The boatman lit the candle of a little square lantern and set it in the bottom of the boat. The musicians made some preliminary chords and conversed about being in tune.

Tall trees of some poplar variety that always resemble hearse plumes dotted the plain to the westward and, as the uproar of colors there faded to a subtle rose, their black solemn outlines intervened like bars across this pink and pallor. A wind, cool and fragrant, reminiscent of flowers and grass and lakes, came from those mystic shadows—places whence the two silver peaks had vanished. The boatman held his pole under his arm while he swiftly composed a cigarette.

The musicians played slumberously. We did not wish to hear any too well. It was better to lie and watch the large stars come out and let the music be merely a tale of the past, a recital from the possessions of one's own memory, an invoking of other songs, other nights. For, after all, the important part of these dreamful times to the wanderer is that they cry to him with emotional and tender voices of his past. The yellow glitter of the lantern at the boatman's feet made his shadow to be a black awful thing that hung angrily over us. There was a sudden shrill yell from the darkness. There had almost been a collision. In the blue velvet of the sky, the stars had gathered in thousands.

14. Above all Things

City of Mexico,
Above all things, the stranger finds the occupations of foreign peoples to be trivial and inconsequent. The average mind utterly fails to comprehend the new point of view and that such and such a man should be satisfied to carry bundles or mayhap sit and ponder in the sun all his life in this faraway country seems an abnormally stupid thing. The visitor feels scorn. He swells with a knowledge of his geographical experience. "How futile are the lives of these people," he remarks, "and what incredible ignorance that they should not be aware of their futility." This is the arrogance of the man who has not yet solved himself and discovered his own actual futility.

Yet, indeed, it requires wisdom to see a brown woman in one garment crouched listlessly in the door of a low adobe hut while a naked brown baby sprawls on his stomach in the dust of the roadway—it requires wisdom to see this thing and to see it a million times and yet to say: "Yes, this is important to the scheme of nature. This is part of her economy. It would not be well if it had never been."

It perhaps might be said—if any one dared—that the most worthless literature of the world has been that which has been written by the men of one nation concerning the men of another.

It seems that a man must not devote himself for a time to attempts at psychological perception. He can be sure of two things, form and color. Let him then see all he can but let him not sit in literary judgment on this or that manner of the people. Instinctively he will feel that there are similarities but he will encounter many little gestures, tones, tranquilities, rages, for which his blood, adjusted to another temperature, can possess no interpreting power. The strangers will be indifferent where he expected passion; they will be passionate where he expected calm. These subtle variations will fill him with contempt.

At first it seemed to me the most extraordinary thing that the lower classes of Indians in this country should insist upon existence at all. Their squalor, their ignorance, seemed so absolute that death—no matter what it has in store—would appear as freedom, joy.

The people of the slums of our own cities fill a man with awe. That vast army with its countless faces immovably cynical, that vast army that silently confronts eternal defeat, it makes one afraid. One listens for the first thunder of the rebellion, the moment when this silence shall be broken by a roar of war. Meanwhile one fears this class, their numbers, their wickedness, their might—even their laughter. There is a vast national respect for them. They have it in their power to become terrible. And their silence suggests everything.

They are becoming more and more capable of defining their condition and this increase of knowledge evinces itself in the deepening of those savage and scornful lines which extend from near the nostrils to the corners of the mouth. It is very distressing to observe this growing appreciation of the situation.

I am venturing to say that this appreciation does not exist in the lower classes of Mexico. No, I am merely going to say that I cannot perceive any evidence of it. I take this last position in order to preserve certain handsome theories which I advanced in the fore part of the article.

It is so human to be envious that of course even these Indians have envied everything from the stars of the sky to the birds, but you cannot ascertain that they feel at all the modern desperate rage at the accident of birth. Of course the Indian can imagine himself a king but he does not apparently feel that there is an injustice in the fact that he was not born a king any more than there is in his not being born a giraffe.

As far as I can perceive him, he is singularly meek and submissive. He has not enough information to be unhappy over his state. Nobody seeks to provide him with it. He is born, he works, he worships, he dies, all on less money than would buy a thoroughbred Newfoundland dog and who dares to enlighten him? Who dares cry out to him that there are plums, plums, plums in the world which belong to him? For my part, I think the apostle would take a formidable responsibility. I would remember that there really was no comfort in the plums after all as far as I had seen them and I would esteem no orations concerning the glitter of plums.

A man is at liberty to be virtuous in almost any position of life. The virtue of the rich is not so superior to the virtue of the poor that we can say that the rich have a great advantage. These Indians are by far the most poverty-stricken class with which I have met but they are not morally the lowest by any means. Indeed, as far as the mere form of religion goes, they are one of the highest. They are exceedingly devout, worshipping with a blind faith that counts a great deal among the theorists.

But according to my view this is not the measure of them. I measure their morality by what evidences of peace and contentment I can detect in the average countenance.

If a man is not given a fair opportunity to be virtuous, if his environment chokes his moral aspirations, I say that he has got the one important cause of complaint and rebellion against society. Of course it is always possible to be a martyr but then we do not wish to be martyrs. Martyrdom offers no inducements to the average mind. We prefer to be treated with justice and then martyrdom is not required. I never could appreciate those grey old gentlemen of history. Why did not they run? I would have run like mad and still respected myself and my religion.

I have said then that a man has the right to rebel if he is not given a fair opportunity to be virtuous. Inversely then, if he possesses this fair opportunity, he cannot rebel, he has no complaint. I am of the opinion that poverty of itself is no cause. It is something above and beyond. For example, there is Collis P. Huntington and William D. Rockefeller—as virtuous as these gentlemen are, I would not say that their virtue is any ways superior to mine for instance. Their opportunities are no greater. They can give more, deny themselves more, in quantity but not relatively. We can each give all that we possess and there I am at once their equal.

I do not think however that they would be capable of sacrifices that would be possible to me. So then I envy them nothing. Far from having a grievance against them, I feel that they will confront an ultimate crisis that I, through my opportunities, may altogether avoid. There is in fact no advantage of importance which I can perceive them possessing over me.

It is for these reasons that I refuse to commit judgment upon these lower classes of Mexico. I even refuse to pity them. It is true that at night many of them sleep in heaps in doorways, and spend their days squatting upon the pavements. It is true that their clothing is scant and thin. All manner of things of this kind are true but yet their faces have almost a certain smoothness, a certain lack of pain, a serene faith. I can feel the superiority of their contentment.

Mexican Tales

15. The Voice of the Mountain

The old man Popocatapetl was seated on a high rock with his white mantle about his shoulders. He looked at the sky, he looked at the sea, he looked at the land—nowhere could he see any food. And he was very hungry, too.

Who can understand the agony of a creature whose stomach is as large as a thousand churches, when this same stomach is as empty as a broken water jar?

He looked longingly at some islands in the sea. "Ah, those flat cakes! If I had them." He stared at storm-clouds in the sky. "Ah what a drink is there." But the King of Everything, you know, had forbidden the old man Popocatapetl to move at all because he feared that every footprint would make a great hole in the land. So the old fellow was obliged to sit still and wait for his food to come within reach. Anyone who has tried this plan knows what intervals lie between meals.

Once his friend, the little eagle, flew near and Popocatapetl called to him. "Ho, tiny bird, come and consider with me as to how I shall be fed."

The little eagle came and spread his legs apart and considered manfully, but he could do nothing with the situation. "You see," he said, "this is no ordinary hunger which one goat will suffice—"

Popocatapetl groaned an assent.

"—but it is an enormous affair," continued the little eagle, "which requires something like a dozen stars. I don't see what can be done unless we get that little creature of the earth—that little animal with two arms, two legs, one head and a very brave air, to invent something. He is said to be very wise.

MEXICAN TALES. | [rule] | BY STEPHEN CRANE. | [rule] | The Voice of the Mountain. | Copyright 1895 by Bacheller, Johnson & Bacheller.

"Who claims it for him?" asked Popocatapetl.

"'He claims it for himself," responded the eagle.

"Well, summon him! Let us see! He is doubtless a kind little animal and when he sees my distress he will invent something."

"Good!" The eagle flew until he discovered one of these small creatures. "Oh, tiny animal, the great chief Popocatapetl summons you!"

"Does he indeed?"

"Popocatapetl, the great chief," said the eagle again, thinking that the little animal had not heard rightly.

"Well, and why does he summon me?"

"Because he is in distress and he needs your assistance."

The little animal reflected for a time and then said: "I will go!"

When Popocatapetl perceived the little animal and the eagle he stretched forth his great solemn arms. "Oh, blessed little animal with two arms, two legs, a head, and a very brave air, help me in my agony. Behold, I, Popocatapetl, who saw the King of Everything fashioning the stars, I, who knew the sun in his childhood, I, Popocatapetl, appeal to you, little animal. I am hungry."

After a while the little animal asked: "How much will you pay?"

"Pay?" said Popocatapetl.

"Pay?" said the eagle.

"Assuredly," quoth the little animal. " 'Pay'!"

"But," demanded Popocatapetl, "were you never hungry? I tell you I am hungry and is your first word then 'pay'?"

The little animal turned coldly away. "Oh, Popocatapetl, how much wisdom has flown past you since you saw the King of Everything fashioning the stars and since you knew the sun in his childhood? I said 'pay' and moreover your distress measures my price. It is our law. Yet it is true that we did not see the King of Everything fashioning the stars. Nor did we know the sun in his childhood."

Then did Popocatapetl roar and shake in his rage. "Oh, louse—louse—louse! Let us bargain then! How much for your blood?" Over the head of the little animal hung death.

But he instantly bowed himself and prayed: "Popocatapetl, the great, you who saw the King of Everything fashioning the stars and who knew the sun in his childhood, forgive this poor little animal. Your sacred hunger shall be my care. I am your servant."

"It is well," said Popocatapetl at once, for his spirit was ever kindly. "And now what will you do?"

The little animal put his hand upon his chin and reflected. "Well, it seems you are hungry and the King of Everything has forbidden you to go for food in fear that your monstrous feet will riddle the earth with holes. What you need is a pair of wings."

"A pair of wings!" cried Popocatapetl delightedly.

"A pair of wings!" screamed the eagle in joy.

"How very simple, after all!"

"And yet how wise!"

"But," said Popocatapetl, after the first outburst, "who can make me these wings?"

The little animal replied: "I and my kind are great, because at times we can make one mind control a hundred thousand bodies. This is the secret of our performances. It will be nothing for us to make wings for even you, great Popocatapetl. I and my kind will come"—continued the crafty little animal—"we will come and dwell on this beautiful plain that stretches from the sea to the sea and we will make wings for you."

Popocatapetl wished to embrace the little animal. "Oh, glorious! Oh, best of little brutes! Run! run! run! Summon your kind, dwell in the plain and make me wings. Ah, when once Popocatapetl can soar on his wings from star to star, then indeed—"

o o o o · o o

Poor old stupid Popocatapetl! The little animal summoned his kind, they dwelt on the plains, they made this and they made that, but they made no wings for Popocatapetl.

And sometimes when the thunderous voice of the old peak rolls and rolls, if you know that tongue, you can hear him say: "Oh, traitor! Traitor! Traitor! Where are my wings? My wings, traitor! I am hungry! Where are my wings?"

But this little animal merely places his finger beside his nose and winks.

"Your wings, indeed, fool! Sit still and howl for them! Old idiot!"

16.   How the Donkey Lifted the Hills

Many people suppose that the donkey is lazy. This is a great mistake. It is his pride.

Years ago, there was nobody quite so fine as the donkey. He was a great swell in those times. No one could express an opinion of anything without the donkey showing him where he was wrong in it. No one could mention the name of an important personage without the donkey declaring how well he knew him.

The donkey was above all things a proud and aristocratic beast.

One day a party of animals were discussing one thing and another, until finally the conversation drifted around to mythology.

"I have always admired that giant, Atlas," observed the ox in the course of the conversation. "It was amazing how he could carry things."

"Oh, yes, Atlas," said the donkey. "I knew him very well. I once met a man and we got talking of Atlas. I expressed my admiration for the giant and my desire to meet him some day, if possible. Whereupon the man said that there was nothing quite so easy. He was sure that his dear friend, Atlas, would be happy to meet so charming a donkey. Was I at leisure next Monday? Well, then, could I dine with him upon that date? So, you see, it was all arranged. I found Atlas to be a very pleasant fellow."

MEXICAN TALES. | [rule] | BY STEPHEN CRANE. | [rule] | How the Donkey Lifted the Hills. | [Copyright 1895.]

"It has always been a wonder to me how he could have carried the earth on his back," said the horse.

"Oh, my dear sir, nothing is more simple," cried the donkey. "One has only to make up one's mind to it and then—do it. That is all. I am quite sure that if I wished I could carry a range of mountains upon my back."

All the others said, "Oh, my!"

"Yes I could," asserted the donkey, stoutly. "It is merely a question of making up one's mind. I will bet."

"I will wager also," said the horse. "I will wager my ears that you can't carry a range of mountains upon your back."

"Done," cried the donkey.

Forthwith the party of animals set out for the mountains. Suddenly, however, the donkey paused and said: "Oh, but look here! Who will place this range of mountains upon my back? Surely I cannot be expected to do the loading also."

Here was a great question. The party consulted. At length the ox said: "We will have to ask some men to shovel the mountains upon the donkey's back."

Most of the others clapped their hoofs or their paws and cried: "Ah, that is the thing."

The horse, however, shook his head doubtfully. "I don't know about these men. They are very sly. They will introduce some deviltry into the affair."

"Why, how silly," saiid the donkey. "Apparently you do not understand men. They are the most gentle, guileless creatures."

"Well," retorted the horse, "I will doubtless be able to escape since I am not to be encumbered with any mountains. Proceed."

The donkey smiled in derision at these observations by the horse.

Presently they came upon some men who were laboring away like mad, digging ditches, felling trees, gathering fruits, carrying water, building huts.

"Look at these men, would you," said the horse. "Can you trust them after this exhibition of their depravity? See how each one selfishly—"

The donkey interrupted with a loud laugh.

"What nonsense!"

And then he cried out to the men: "Ho, my friends, will you please come and shovel a range of mountains upon my back?"

"What?"

"Will you please come and shovel a range of mountains upon my back?"

The men were silent for a time. Then they went apart and debated. They gesticulated a great deal.

Some apparently said one thing and some another. At last they paused and one of their number came forward.

"Why do you wish a range of mountains shovelled upon you back?"

"It is a wager," cried the donkey.

The men consulted again. And, as the discussion became older, their heads went closer and closer together, until they merely whispered, and did not gesticulate at all. Ultimately they cried: "Yes, certainly we will shovel a range of mountains upon your back for you."

"Ah, thanks," said the donkey.

"Here is surely some deviltry," said the horse behind his hoof to the ox.

The entire party proceeded then to the mountains. The donkey drew a long breath and braced his legs.

"Are you ready?" asked the men.

"All ready," cried the donkey.

The men began to shovel.

The dirt and the stones flew over the donkey's back in showers. It was not long before his legs were hidden. Presently only his neck and head remained in view. Then at last this wise donkey vanished. There had been made no great effect upon the range of mountains. They still towered toward the sky.

The watching crowd saw the heap of dirt and stones make a little movement and then was heard a muffled cry. "Enough! Enough! It was not two ranges of mountains. The wager was for one range of mountains. It is not fair! It is not fair!"

But the new men only laughed as they shovelled on.

"Enough! Enough! Oh, woe is me—thirty snow-capped peaks

upon my little back. Ah, these false, false men. Oh, virtuous, wise and holy men, desist."

The men again laughed. They were as busy as fiends with their shovels.

"Ah, brutal, cowardly, accursed men, ah, good, gentle and holy men, please remove some of those damnable peaks. I will adore your beautiful shovels forever. I will be a slave to the beckoning of your little fingers. I will no longer be my own donkey—I will be your donkey."

The men burst into a triumphant shout and ceased shovelling.

"Swear it, mountain-carrier!"

"I swear! I swear! I swear!"

The other animals scampered away then, for these men in their plots and plans were very terrible. "Poor old foolish fellow," cried the horse; "he may keep his ears. He will need them to hear and count the blows that are now to fall upon him."

The men unearthed the donkey. They beat him with their shovels. "Ho, come on, slave." Encrusted with earth, yellow-eyed from fright, the donkey limped towards his prison. His ears hung down like the leaves of the plantain during the great rain.

So now, when you see a donkey with a church, a palace, and three villages upon his back, and he goes with infinite slowness, moving but one leg at a time, do not think him lazy. It is his pride.

17. The Victory of the moon

The Strong Man of the Hills lost his wife. Immediately he went abroad calling aloud. The people all crouched afar in the dark of their huts and cried to him when he was yet a long distance away.

THE VICTORY OF THE MOON | [rule] | BY STEPHEN CRANE: | [rule] |
[Copyright, 1895.]

"No, no; Great Chief, we have not even seen the imprint of your wife's sandal in the sand. If we had seen it, you would have found us bowed down in worship before the marks of her ten glorious brown toes for we are but poor devils of Indians and the grandeur of the sun's rays on her hair would have turned our eyes to dust."

"Her toes are not brown. They are pink." said the Strong Man from the Hills. "Therefore do I believe that you speak truth when you say you have not seen her, good little men of the valley. In this matter of her great loveliness, however, you speak a little too strongly. As she is no longer among my possessions, I have no mind to hear her praised. Whereabouts is the best man of you?"

None of them had stomach for this honor at the time. They surmised that the Strong Man of the Hills had some plan for combat, and they knew that the best man of them would have in this encounter only the strength of the meat in the grip of the fire. "Great King," they said in one voice, "there is no best man here."

"How is this?" roared the Strong Man. "There must be one who excels. It is a law. Let him step forward then."

But they solemnly shook their heads. "There is no best man here."

The Strong Man turned upon them so furiously that many fell to the ground. "There must be one. Let him step forward." Shivering, they huddled together and tried, in their fear, to thrust each other toward the Strong Man.

At this time a young philosopher approached the throng slowly. The philosophers of that age were all young men in the full heat of life. The old greybeards were, for the most part, very stupid, and were so accounted.

"Strong Man from the Hills," said the young philosopher, "go to yonder brook and bathe. Then come and eat of this fruit. Then gaze for a time at the blue sky and the green earth. Afterwards I have something to say to you."

"You are not so wise that I am obliged to bathe before listening to you?" demanded the Strong Man, insolently.

"No," said the young philosopher. All the people thought this reply very strange.

"Why, then, must I bathe and eat of fruit and gaze at the earth and the sky?"

"Because they are pleasant things to do."

"Have I, do you think, any thirst at this time for pleasant things?"

"Bathe, eat, gaze," said the young philosopher with a gesture.

The Strong Man did indeed whirl his bronzed and terrible limbs in the silver water. Then he lay in the shadow of a tree and ate the cool fruit and gazed at the sky and the earth. "This is a fine comfort," he said. After a time he suddenly struck his forehead with his finger. "By the way, did I tell you that my wife had fled from me?"

"I knew it," said the young philosopher.

Later the Strong Man slept peacefully. The young philosopher smiled.

But in the night the little men of the valley came clamoring: "Oh, Strong Man of the Hills, the moon derides you!"

The philosopher went to them in the darkness. "Be still little people. It is nothing. The derision of the moon is nothing."

But the little men of the valley would not cease their uproar. "Oh, Strong Man! Strong Man, awake! Awake! The moon derides you!"

Then the Strong Man aroused and shook his locks away from his eyes. "What is it, good little men of the valley?"

"Oh, Strong Man, the moon derides you! Oh, Strong Man!"

The Strong Man looked and there indeed was the moon laughing down at him. He sprang to his feet and roared: "Ah, old fat lump of a moon, you laugh? Have you then my wife?"

The moon said no word, but merely smiled in a way that was like a flash of silver bars.

"Well, then, moon, take this home to her," thundered the Strong Man, and he hurled his spear.

The moon clapped both hands to its eye and cried, "Oh! Oh!"

The little people of the valley cried, "Oh, this terrible Strong Man! He has smitten our sacred moon in the eye!"

The young philosopher cried nothing at all.

The Strong Man threw his coat of crimson feathers upon the

ground. He took his knife and felt its edge. "Look you, philosopher," he said. "I have lost my wife, and yet the bath, the meal of fruit in the shade, the sight of sky and earth are still good to me, but when this false moon derides me there must be a killing."

"I understand you," said the young philosopher. The Strong Man ran off into the night. The little men of the valley clapped their hands in ecstacy and terror. "Ah, ah! What a battle there will be!"

The Strong Man went into his own hills and gathered there many great rocks and trunks of trees. It was strange to see him erect upon a peak of the mountains and hurling these things at the moon. He kept the air full of them.

"Fat moon, come closer!" he shouted. "Come closer, and let it be my knife against your knife. Oh, to think we are obliged to tolerate such an old, fat, stupid, lazy, good-for-nothing moon! You are ugly as death, while I— Oh, moon, you stole my beloved, and it was nothing, but when you stole my beloved and laughed at me, it became another matter. And yet you are so ugly, so fat, so stupid, so lazy, so good-for-nothing. Ah, I shall go mad! Come closer, moon, and let me examine your round, gray skull with this club."

And he always kept the air full of great missiles.

The moon merely laughed, and said: "Why should I come closer?"

Wildly did the Strong Man pile rock upon rock. He built him a tower that was the father of all towers. It made the mountains appear to be babes. Upon the summit of it he swung his great club and flourished his knife

The little men by the valley far below beheld a great storm and at the end of it they said: "Look, the moon is dead!" The cry went to and fro on the earth: "The moon is dead!"

The Strong Man went to the home of the moon. She, the sought one, lay upon a cloud and her little foot dangled over the side of it. The Strong Man took this little foot in his two hands and kissed it. "Ah, beloved!" he moaned, "I would rather this little foot was upon my dead neck than that moon should ever have the privilege of seeing it."

She leaned over the edge of the cloud and gazed at him. "How dusty you are! Why do you puff so? Veritably, you are an ordinary person. Why did I ever find you interesting?"

The Strong Man flung his knife into the air and turned back toward the earth. "If the young philosopher had been at my elbow," he reflected bitterly, "I would have doubtless have gone at the matter in another way. What does my strength avail me in this contest?"

The battered moon, limping homeward, replied to the Strong Man from the Hills: "Aye, surely! My weakness is in this thing as strong as your strength. I am victor with my ugliness, my age, my stoutness, my stupidity, my laziness, my good-for-nothingness. Woman is woman. Men are equal in everything save good fortune. I envy you not."

Textual Afterword

Textual Afterword

The textual history of the articles in this book is complex and, at present, only partially known. Stephen Crane undoubtedly wrote them all either during his trip or soon after it ended, but not all of them were distributed by its sponsor, Bacheller, Johnson & Bacheller.

Three sketches—12. "The Main Streets of this City," 13. "The Viga Canal," and 14. "Above All Things"—were left in manuscript when Crane died. Those manuscripts are on cream wove paper measuring 33 × 22.7 centimeters, with thirty-seven horizontal blue rules .9 centimeters apart. Evidently they had been part of a notebook Crane carried with him on the trip. The separated leaves are among the Stephen and Cora Crane papers once known as the Bohnenberger-Hill Collection, which was acquired in 1952 by the Butler Library of Columbia University. Until they were published (with errors in transcription) in R. W. Stallman's "Stephen Crane: Some New Sketches" (*Bulletin of the New York Public Library*, LXXI [November 1967], 554–562), only parts of "Above All Things" had seen print: Stallman and Lillian Gilkes, eds., *Stephen Crane: Letters* (New York, 1960), p. 55, annotated a letter with a deficient text made up of excerpts from paragraphs thirteen and fourteen; and scattered sentences were drawn together from various points to form a composite passage in Maurice Bassan, ed., *Stephen Crane's Maggie[:] Text and Context* (Belmont, California, 1966), p. 96. The three sketches are here printed from the manuscripts.

It also is unlikely that Bacheller, Johnson & Bacheller saw either of two other sketches: 5. "Galveston, Texas, in 1895" or 6. "Patriot Shrine of Texas." Cora Crane almost certainly was responsible for publishing the Galveston sketch in the *Westminster Gazette*, 6 November 1900, pp. 1–2, reprinted here. By then Crane had been dead almost exactly five months, and Irving Bacheller had been out of the syndicate business for some years. In 1900 his *Eben Holden* was published, and he was well on his way to a career as a popular novelist. "Galveston, Texas, in 1895" was first reprinted in Olov W. Fryckstedt, ed., *Stephen Crane: Uncollected Writings* (Uppsala, 1963), pp. 144–149. The San Antonio sketch appeared as "Patriot Shrine of Texas" in the Omaha *Daily Bee*, 8 January 1899, p. 15, reprinted here, and the Omaha *Weekly Bee*, 11 January 1899, p. 12, and as "Stephen Crane in Texas" in the Pittsburgh *Leader*, 8 January 1899, p. 23. It was reprinted by Bernice Slote as "San Antonio" in *Prairie Schooner*, LXIII (Summer 1969), 176–183.

Bacheller, Johnson & Bacheller did distribute the remaining twelve articles to its subscribing newspapers. Six of them survive in the galley proofs that were one form in which the syndicate released them: 1. "Nebraska's Bitter Fight for Life"[1]; 2. "Seen at Hot Springs"; 3. "Grand Opera in New Orleans"; 4. "The Fête of Mardi Gras"; 7. "Stephen Crane in Mexico: I"; 9. "In Free Silver Mexico." They are here reprinted from those proofs preserved by Crane in scrapbooks now in the Butler Library.

The remaining six articles are reprinted here from appearances in the Nebraska *State Journal*, a newspaper that often used the stereotype plates or mats that were another form in which the syndicate supplied its work: 8. "Stephen Crane in Mexico: II," 19 May 1895, p. 13; 10. "A Jag of Pulque is Heavy," 12 August 1895, p. 5; 11. "The Dress of Old Mexico," 18 October 1896, p. 9; 15. "The Voice of the Mountain," 22 May 1895, p. 4; 16. "How the Donkey Lifted the Hills;" 6 June 1895, p. 4; 17. "The Victory of the Moon," 24 July 1895, p. 4. Note that articles 15 and 16 appeared in the *State Journal* under the series title "Mexican Tales." When Irving Bacheller was editor of the *Pocket Magazine* he first reprinted articles 15, 16, and 17—without the series title—in III (November

---

[1]Crane had pasted this proof sheet in his scrapbook, but at some time the last portion worked loose. Only part of it now survives. Accordingly, copy-text for this edition has been the surviving portions of the proof sheet, with the missing portion supplied from the Nebraska *State Journal* appearance: 41.1–46.8 (< ... > upon the mes-) and 49.16 (take me < ... >) -51.35 are from the proof sheet; 46.8 (quite prairies) -49.16 (They) are from Nebraska *State Journal*, 24 February 1895, p. 14.

1896), 136–142; IV (June 1897), 144–151; and V (July 1897), 144–152. All three articles later were collected—again without the series title—by Cora Crane in *Last Words* (London, 1902).[2] Fryckstedt's *Stephen Crane: Uncollected Writings*, pp. 121–144, 149–170, first reprinted articles 1–4 and 7–11.

Students of Crane's work will find that both the titles and the texts of many articles printed here vary from their appearances in Fryckstedt's collection and Ames W. Williams' and Vincent Starrett's *Stephen Crane: A Bibliography* (Glendale, 1948). Such variation must be expected with syndicated material. The three surviving manuscripts suggest that Crane sent his dispatches to the syndicate untitled, without internal headings, and with incomplete datelines. The syndicate releases he preserved indicate that the syndicate edited the work hastily, supplying titles they thought would attract attention and dates they found suited to the dates on which they wanted the pieces published by subscribers. Usually these dates had little relation to the date on which Crane visited a place; often the dates were out of sequence with the order of his itinerary. (Release dates survive for three sketches: "The Fête of Mardi Gras" was "For Feb. 16."; the first "Stephen Crane in Mexico" was "For July 21."; and "In Free Silver Mexico" was "For June 30.") Subscribing newspapers, however, did as they pleased with what they bought: they ignored release dates, changed titles, datelines, and texts, inserted internal subheadings of their own, and often omitted the syndicate's copyright notice. The result of all this is a bibliographical and textual complexity that has made this area of Crane studies imperfect not only textually and bibliographically, but also biographically and critically. Some indication of the degree of that complexity may be apparent in the following chart of the appearances of the syndicated travel sketches examined during the preparation of this edition.

---

[2]There are typescripts of the Mexican Tales (15, 16, and 17) in the Alderman Library, and the Butler Library has carbon copies of those typescripts for 16 and 17. But they can be assigned no authority: Cora prepared them, almost certainly after Crane's death, probably for the American publication of *Last Words*, and undoubtedly from clippings of early publications.

1. "Nebraska's Bitter Fight for Life"
    a. New Orleans *Times-Democrat*, 23 February 1895, as "Nebraska's Fight"
    b. Nebraska *State Journal*, 24 February 1895, p. 14, as "Waiting for the Spring"
    c. Galveston *Daily News*, 24 February 1895, p. 10, as "A Fight for Life"
    d. New York *Press*, 24 February 1895, p. 2, as "A State's Hard Fight"
    e. Philadelphia *Press*, 24 February 1895, part 3, p. 25, as "Nebraskans' Bitter Fight for Life"

2. "Seen at Hot Springs
    a. Nebraska *State Journal*, 3 March 1895, p. 10
    b. Galveston *Daily News*, 3 March 1895, p. 4, as "Hot Springs Scenes"
    c. Philadelphia *Press*, 3 March 1895, part 3, p. 29, as "The Merry Throngs at Hot Springs"

3. "Grand Opera in New Orleans"
    a. Nebraska *State Journal*, 24 March 1895, p. 11, as "Opera in New Orleans"
    b. Philadelphia *Press*, 24 March 1895, part 3, p. 25
    c. Galveston *Daily News*, 25 March 1895, p. 4, as "A Century of Music"

4. "The Fête of Mardi Gras"
    a. Philadelphia *Press*, 16 February 1896, p. 30, as "Mardi Gras . . . Festival"
    b. Nebraska *State Journal*, 16 February 1896, p. 11
    c. Cincinnati *Commercial Gazette*, 23 February 1896, p. 19

7. "Stephen Crane in Mexico"
    a. Nebraska *State Journal*, 21 July 1895, p. 13
    b. Philadelphia *Press*, 21 July 1895, p. 32, as "Ancient Capital of Montezuma"
    c. Galveston *Daily News*, 21 July 1895, p. 10, as "From Stephen Crane"

8. "Stephen Crane in Mexico"
    a. Nebraska *State Journal*, 19 May 1895, p. 13
    b. Galveston *Daily News*, 19 May 1895, p. 13, as "Crane Sees Mexico"
    c. Philadelphia *Press*, 19 May 1895, p. 33, as "Mexican Sights and Street Scenes"

9. "In Free Silver Mexico"
   a. Nebraska *State Journal*, 30 June 1895, p. 13
   b. Philadelphia *Press*, 30 June 1895, p. 31, as "Free Silver Down in Mexico"
   c. Galveston *Daily News*, 1 July 1895, p. 4, as "Free Silver Mexico"

10. "A Jag of Pulque is Heavy"
    a. Philadelphia *Press*, 11 August 1895, p. 26, as "Jags of Pulque Down in Mexico"
    b. Nebraska *State Journal*, 12 August 1895, p. 5

11. "The Dress of Old Mexico"
    a. Nebraska *State Journal*, 18 October 1896, p. 9
    b. Philadelphia *Press*, 18 October 1896, p. 34, as "Hats, Shirts and Spurs in Mexico"
    c. San Francisco *Chronicle*, 18 October 1896, p. 12, as "Hats, Shirts and Spurs"

The titles of those dispatches in this edition are taken from the copy-texts. Three have been emended slightly: the circumflex accent was supplied in 4, "The Fête of Mardi Gras," and differentiating numerals I and II have been added in 7 and 8, the two articles headed "Stephen Crane in Mexico." The titles of the pieces represented by surviving syndicate releases are authoritative; they should supplant the variant titles, supplied by individual newspapers, by which some are known.

Copy-texts were emended only where some feature of the text clearly demanded correction. There were five general situations that evoked emendation. The first comprised probable printer's errors. Among these are replications (1:3.7–8), omissions (1:6.36), substitutions (3:22.17), and wrong pointings (7:42.21). The second class is of indisputable solecisms, whatever the source. These include blunders such as Crane's *it's* for *its* (12:68.22), and his unsanctioned spellings of proper nouns (1:6.26), common English words (12:69.9), and foreign words (6:40.20), as well as his uncertain practice in handling the grammatical functions of the comma (1:7.13). The third class is of departures from Crane's invariable practices of spelling and word division, when these are acceptable alternatives. Among these are *traveler* for *traveller* (8:55.19), -*our*

for *-or* (5:31.14), and *sidewalks* for *side-walks* (4:24.13)—all variations from Crane's habitual usage, and none apparently authorial
in source. The fourth class consists of inconsistencies in practices
within a work. For example, in "Nebraska's Bitter Fight for Life"
the word *state* generally is capitalized from the beginning to 11.28,
from which point it is begun with lower-case. Evidently, a non-
authorial influence decided either one practice or the other—if not
both. But regularization has not been imposed from work to work,
unless there is evidence that a clear authorial preference has been
violated. So *trolly-cars* appears in 5:31.26, but there is *trolley cars*
in 6:36.13. The fifth general class in which emendation has been
applied consists of the appurtenances devised by the syndicate or
its subscribers for Crane's texts. They have been treated in three
ways: decks, the series of attention-getting statements immediately
following a title, and copyright notices have been transcribed in
notes near the beginning of each work; sub-headings have been
recorded in the table of emendations below; and ornamental initials and captions for illustrations have been dropped without
comment. No other silent emendations have been made.

   The following table records all editorial emendations of copy-
texts other than the class of silent deletions. The sigla are conventional: a reading to the left of a bracket (]) is from the copy-text, to
the right is from this edition; a bar (|) indicates a line ending; a
series of three points within angle brackets < ... > indicates unaffected words in a report of emended features; a paragraph sign (¶)
indicates the beginning of a new paragraph; a wavy dash (∽)
replaces a word in this edition corresponding to the word in the
copy text associated with emended pointing; and an inferior caret
(∧) indicates either the absence of pointing in the copy-text when
pointing is supplied in this edition, or the deletion of pointing in
this edition when it is present in the copy-text.

1. "Nebraska's Bitter Fight for Life"

3.4   east] East
3.6   State] state (Note that the copy-text practice changes
               at 11.28.)

3.7–8	sufficient. | east have made it appear that the entire State of Nebraska is a desert. In reality the situation is serious, but it does not include the whole State. However, people feel that thirty counties in pain and destitution is sufficient. |¶ The] sufficient. ¶ The
3.8	State] state
4.35	window∧] ∽,
5.2	traveling] travelling
6.2	States] states
6.25	States] states
6.26	Halcombe] Holcomb (Silas Alexander Holcomb governed Nebraska from 1894 to 1899—*DAB*.)
6.36	correspnds with railrads] corresponds with railroads
7.4	faceteous < · · · > east] facetious < · · · > East
7.12	east] East
7.13	people∧] ∽ —
7.17	States] states
7.28	State's] state's
7.30	State] state
7.31	east] East
8.3	yeh.'] ∽."
8.10	States] states
8.33	uncomprising] uncompromising
8.36	legislature∧] ∽,
9.12	Lincoln∧] ∽,
9.27	sod houses] sod-houses (Compare 9.24.)
9.34	sidewalk] side-walk (Compare 12:66.21–22.)
10.4	men∧] ∽,
10.8	chinmey] chimney
10.25	wich] which
10.35	'em out out] 'em out
11.5	then] ,
11.12	connot] cannot
11.23	part∧] ∽,
11.24	winds,] ∽∧
11.27	phenominal] phenomenal

11.36   eastern] Eastern
12.6   away,] ∽ ∧
12.7   said ∧] ∽ :
12.13–14   Who the | "How do you get along?"] Who the hell
               told you I did get along?" (Emendation based on the
               Nebraska *State Journal* appearance. In other exam-
               ined appearances the interviewer simply is answered,
               "'Don't git along, stranger.'")
12.25   Holcombe] Holcomb
12.32   ∧This] ∽ "
13.15   River] river (Compare 3.11 in the text, and see also
               note 3.6.)

2. "Seen at Hot Springs"
15.5   feeling ∧] ∽ ,
15.15   tracts ∧] ∽ ,
16.11   eastern] Eastern
16.19   nd] and
17.31   Springs] springs
17.35   they ∧] ∽ ,
18.28   stranger ∧] ∽ ,
19.3   traveller,] ∽ ∧
19.22   stranger ∧] ∽ ,
19.28   you] You
19.32   anguish,] ∽ ∧
19.34   stranger ∧] ∽ ,

3. "Grand Opera in New Orleans"
20.6   city,] ∽ ∧
20.9   scared] scarred
20.13   roofs,] ∽ ∧
21.6   Domingo,] ∽ ∧
21.8–9   theatre,] ∽ ∧
21.18   said,] ∽ ∧
21.23   opera-house] opera house (Compare 20.11.)
21.34   baritone∧] ∽ ,

22.17   thrones] thorns
22.28   Chavaroach] Chavaroche (Emendation based on arti-
             cles and advertisements in the New Orleans *Times-
             Democrat*, 20 February 1895. The name is spelled
             correctly in the caption of the Kauffman drawing that
             illustrates this sketch.)
23.3   ingrossed] engrossed
23.12   Armours < ... > Dragon de Villar] Amours < ... >
             Dragons de Villars
23.34   can be] can see

4. "The Fête of Mardi Gras"
24.13   sidewalks] side-walks
24.14   where∧too] ∽ , ∽ ,
24.21   where∧] ∽,
25.11   boys∧] ∽,
25.21   street∧ cars] street-cars (Compare 13:70.25 and
             70.31.)
25.29   street∧car] street-car
25.32   cossack] Cossack
26.6   street∧cars] street-cars
26.16   an∧] ∽'
26.17   gettin,] ∽'
26.27   minstrels∧] ∽ ,
26.29   street∧ cars] street-cars
26.36   raiment∧] ∽,
27.12   time,] ∽ ∧
27.15   dreamed∧] ∽,
28.10   street∧]∽,
28.20   green∧ < ... > sunlight] ∽, < ... > sun-light
             (Compare 2:15.3 and 12:66.22.)
28.24   side, < ... > cloaks∧ and bearing] ∽∧ < ... > ∽,
             bearing
28.26   And∧] ∽,
29.15–16   and∧< ... >death∧like]∽∧< ... >death-like
29.21   out∧displayed] out-displayed

29.22–23   Occasionally∧] ∽,

5. "Galveston, Texas, in 1895"
30.10   resemblances∧] ∽;
30.14   South-Western] south-western
31.8   trays] treys
31.14   colour] color
31.24   colour] color
31.27   clamouring] clamoring
32.24   harbour] harbor
33.13   harbour] harbor
33.34   outskirts remind] outskirts would remind
34.16   colour] color
34.19   colour] color
34.20   type∧] ∽,

6. "Patriot Shrine of Texas"
35.23   you?∧] ∽!"
36.17–18   Ashes of Ambitions.] (Subheading deleted.)
36.28   has] have
37.11–12   Ran Short of Indians.] (Subheading deleted.)
38.9   pretentous] portentous (The Pittsburgh *Leader*
            appearance has "portentious," Crane's usual render-
            ing of "portentous." "Pretentious" would be
            unlikely in context. Compare 12:69 and 13:72.35.)
38.10   fathers∧] ∽,
38.13–14   Literary Aspirants.] (Subheading deleted.)
38.28   silence ∧] ∽,
39.7–8   A Famous Meeting.] (Subheading deleted.)
39.14   Anna] Ana
39.16   Anna] Ana
39.27   or of staying] or staying
40.15   faces ∧] ∽,
40.20   concarne, tomales < ... > frjoles] con carne, tamales
            < ... > frijoles (Compare 7:48.32.)
40.24–25   Around the Town.] (Subheading deleted.)

41.10   general,] ᵕ ∧

7. "Stephen Crane in Mexico: I"

42.1   car-windows] car ∧ windows (Compare 47.25 and 50.33.)
42.21   ∧ yes ∧ or 'Certainly∧ '] 'ᵕ' or 'ᵕ,'
42.23   "up] ∧ ᵕ
42.31   you've] you're
42.35   No.] ᵕ !
42.36   Thunder∧] ᵕ !
43.9   tan-bark,] ᵕ ∧
43.20–21   then ∧ finally∧ < ... > shadow—blue, some one] < ... > shadow-blue, someone
44.5–6   passenger < ... > bird,] passengers < ... > ᵕ ∧
44.13   There-after] Thereafter
46.7   rythmically] rhythmically
46.21   portentiously] portentously
46.30   sage∧brush] sage-brush (Compare 46.33 and 47.36.)
47.2   traveler] traveller
47.9   abining] abiding
47.22   high∧lights] high-lights
47.27   was] were
48.14   travelers] travellers
48.27   Potosi < ... > travelers] Potosí < ... > travellers
48.32   tomales < ... > travelers] tamales < ... > travellers
50.4   Nevada] Nevado
50.18   man ∧] ᵕ,
50.20   haranged] harangued
50.34   man ∧] ᵕ,
51.3   animals ∧] ᵕ,
51.7   before ∧] ᵕ,
51.13   affair ∧] ᵕ,
51.15   mague] maguey

8. "Stephen Crane in Mexico: II"
52.17   sunlight] sun-light

53.15   day∧lights] day-lights
54.13   then ∧] ⌣,
54.27   centre] center
54.36–55.1   STREET VENDERS OF MEXICO.] (Subheading
             deleted.)
55.19   traveler] traveller
55.32   then ∧] ⌣,
55.36   who ∧] ⌣,
56.16   lit- | the] little
57.7 $14∧] $1.

9. "In Free Silver Mexico"
57.20   travelers] travellers
58.12   traveler] traveller
60.7   not supposed] not to be supposed
60.21   tortillas] frijoles

10. "A Jag of Pulque is Heavy"
61.26   circumstaces] circumstances
61.37   minerature] miniature
62.9   shops,] ⌣ ∧
62.21   or ∧] ⌣,
62.23   maguery] maguey
63.1   maquey] maguey
63.3   and] but
63.5   natives,] ⌣ ∧
63.15   combinations ∧] ⌣,

11. "The Dress of Old Mexico"
64.7   sombrerors] sombreros
64.20   he ∧]⌣,
64.25   capital,] ⌣ ∧
64.34   as < ... > enumeration.] at < ... > ⌣:
65.11   senorita] señorita
65.22   country,] ⌣ ∧

65.24   middle ∧ class] middle-class (Compare 9:59.12 and
           59.13.)
66.2   eyes ∧] ∽,
66.4   sky ∧] ∽,
66.7   night ∧]

12. "The Main Streets of this City"

67.3   and, above all,] ∽ ∧ ∽ ∽ ∧
67.21   makes] make
68.4   senorita] señorita
68.22   it's] its
69.7   too ∧] ∽,
69.9   simaltaneous] simultaneous
69.22   told ∧] ∽,
69.24   portentious] portentous

13. "The Viga Canal"

70.6   pulque-shops] pulque∧shops (Compare 70.18 and
           71.33.)
70.8   women ∧] ∽,
70.14   boatman] boatmen
70.16   where ∧] ∽,
71.3   rythmically] rhythmically
71.7   Iztaccihuatl] Ixtaccihuatl
71.8   it's] its
71.12   canoe ∧] ∽,
71.14–15   tomales < ... > clotheing] tamales < ... > clothing
71.20   offers,] ∽ ∧
72.11   it,] ∽ ∧
72.18   locks,] ∽ ∧
72.24   earthern] earthen
72.30   it's] its
72.33   guitarist ∧] ∽,
72.35   portentious] portentous
73.6   and ∧] ∽,
73.9   lakes ∧] ∽,

14. "Above all Things"

75.2	ignorance ∧] ⌣,
75.6	it's] its
75.21	percieve] perceive
75.31	percieve] perceive
76.23	ran] run
76.30	Rockafeller] Rockefeller
76.33	more ∧] ⌣,
77.4	percieve] perceive
77.9	clotheing] clothing
77.31	kind is] kind are

15. "The Voice of the Mountain"

83.11	wings, < ... > oy] ⌣ ! < ... > joy (The exclamation point appropriate to the tonal context appears in *Last Words* [London: Digby, Long & Co., 1902], p. 304.)
83.24	brutes?] ⌣ !
83.26	indeed"—] ⌣ —"

16. "How the Donkey Lifted the Hills"

87.3	fends] fiends

17. "The Victory of the Moon"

88.33	nnt] not
89.32	moou] moon
89.33	this is terrible,] this terrible ∧

In this edition, every possible compound word that extends from the end of one line to the beginning of the next appears as a compound in the middle of a line in the copy-text—except for the following, in which there is coincidental end-of-line hyphenation:

1:6.27–28	rail-|road (railroad)
5:33.25–26	rail-|road (railroad)
7:48.1–2	out-|buildings (out-buildings)

The following compounds and possible compounds extend from the end of one line to the beginning of the next in the copy-texts.

They are reported here in the form in which they are printed in
this edition:

1:3.13	cattlemen
1:9.16	bed-chamber
1:10.9	homestead
1:12.19	car windows (Emended: compare 7:47.25 and 50.33.)
2:19.23	bar-tender
4:27.16	rainbow
4:28.29	far-away
6:36.32	shapeless
6:40.10	wide-brimmed
6:41.3	outskirts
7:43.8	sheep-herder
7:49.3	red-tiled
7:49.11	out-stretched
7:50.30	password
8:52.25	hay-stack
8:53.36	freight-carrying
9:59.26	blue-grass
12:67.5	sun-light
17:90.15	good-for-nothing